MICHAEL LUCAS'S TEN RULES FOR BEING A PORN STAR

1. You have to have the look.

2. You must love sex.

3. You have to want it more than anything.

4. Love yourself tremendously.

5. Have a strong presence.

6. Avoid overexposure.

7. Be flexible.

8. Have a strong personality.

9. Know how to promote yourself.

10. It's all in the attitude.

NAKED

The life and pornography of Michael Lucas

COREY TAYLOR

KENSINGTON BOOKS
http://www.kensingtonbooks.com

KENSINGTON BOOKS are published by

Kensington Publishing Corp.
850 Third Avenue
New York, NY 10022

All Kensington titles, imprints and distributed lines are available at special quantity discounts for bulk purchases for sales promotion, premiums, fund-raising, educational or institutional use.

Special book excerpts or customized printings can also be created to fit specific needs. For details, write or phone the office of the Kensington Special Sales Manager: Kensington Publishing Corp., 850 Third Avenue, New York, NY 10022. Attn. Special Sales Department. Phone: 1-800-221-2647.

Kensington and the K logo Reg. U.S. Pat. & TM Off.

ISBN-13: 978-0-7582-1750-9
ISBN-10: 0-7582-1750-1

First Kensington Trade Paperback Printing: June 2007
10 9 8 7 6 5 4 3 2 1

Printed in the United States of America

. . . for My Immortal

NAKED

Introduction

In his *Life of Johnson*, James Boswell wrote, "This is to me a memorable year; for in it I had the happiness to obtain the acquaintance of that extraordinary man whose memoirs I am now writing; an acquaintance which I shall ever esteem as one of the most fortunate circumstances in my life." The same is true of my experience with Michael Lucas.

Michael Lucas is sexy, generous, and genuine. Because of his no-nonsense approach, he has been described as demanding, conceited, and of course, bitchy. But you don't climb to the top of a multibillion-dollar industry in a country that is foreign to you by always being Mr. Nice Guy. However, if not being a doormat and not letting people take advantage of you means you are bitchy, or if expecting the best from the people you work with or employ means you are bitchy, that's just the way it is. The only people who see that as bitchy are the people who try to take advantage and the people who do not give their best.

Regarding my choice for the title, I took inspiration from the beat novel *Naked Lunch*. In fact, I almost stayed with that, except that the original novel is still so widely read and is, in a literary sense, relatively contemporary in such a way that I did not want the titles to be confused. *Naked Lunch* is about a narcotics addict and the sexual debauchery and depravity of the beat generation.

This story has all of those elements and more. The beat generation, which included such writers as Jack Kerouac and Allen Ginsberg, represented a rebellion against expectations in a similar way as the Romantic Period writers such as Byron and Shelley did. You will find, as I did, that Michael Lucas personifies this same rebellion against expectations. Within his industry, there is no other porn star, producer, or director like him.

The idea of being naked indicates a certain vulnerability. It conjures feelings of complete and utter exposure. Someone who is naked is there for the world to see, is open to the world's judgments, jealousies, kudos, and admiration. This is the way Michael Lucas laid himself out to the process of writing this book and to the world who will now know every inch of him. He allowed unfettered access to his friends, his family, his colleagues and peers, and even his enemies. Michael Lucas is an unapologetic, no-holds-barred kind of man. In this way, too, he is naked, exposed, bare, and honest.

And of course, there is the obvious. He is famous for being *Naked*.

PART ONE

How to Grow a Perfect Porn Star

Because the history of homosexuality has been denied or ignored, omitted in formal historical instruction and given no place in the family-centered oral traditions available to other disenfranchised groups, gay people's hunger for knowledge of their past is strong.

—Martin Duberman

1

"I feel the blood of generations in me," says Michael Lucas, born Andrei Treyvas in Communist Russia in 1972. "I believe that I have this. I think it's a strong survival instinct which is coming from generations of Jews who survived through centuries, through all this terrible persecution and the Holocaust."

The Jewish blood that flows through the veins of this man represents thousands upon thousands of years of non-assimilation. It is an incredibly rich history and probably has more depth than what would be expected of the biggest gay porn star/director/producer of all time. This is the same man who has recently produced the biggest all-male porn film ever: a gay porn version of *Dangerous Liaisons*.

This history, this blood, is very strong and very old. And this is part of what Andrei feels helps him get through his life, which, as you will read, has not always been smooth. Andrei has endured a lot of changes, a lot of traveling, going from continent to continent and from country to country, trying to find the best place to live. This searching has paralleled the journeying that has been done by his Jewish ancestors for centuries. Throughout this journey, Andrei has felt connections through generations with these people who went from Egypt, then who found Israel, then went to Spain, and finally to Russia.

Andrei's direct family line lived in Russia for several generations. Now, Andrei has moved his family to America, as millions of other Jews have done. The history of Jews leaving Russia has now waned, and is essentially over.

In the book *The Soviet Jewish Americans*, Annelise Orleck speaks of a wave of Soviet Jews who came to America in the 1970s. Orleck writes that in 1975, just three years after Andrei was born in Russia, "Elderly immigrant Jews walked slowly arm in arm, speaking an animated mixture of Yiddish and English. Silent old men and women lined the wooden benches facing the sea, silhouetted against a glowing urban night sky."

It wouldn't be long before Andrei's mother would realize that Russia was not the best environment for her son. "I felt that he was not right for the Soviet Union," she says. "I saw that he couldn't live there—his style, everything, was not for Soviet Union. And I was right."

But Andrei's mother, Lena, wasn't the only one who felt her family being called away from Russia. Orleck writes, "After 1967, growing numbers of Soviet Jews demanded the right to emigrate. The loosening of social and cultural restraints during the Khrushchev era had raised many people's hopes and expectations that better times were coming."

Orleck goes on to say that in 1967, Soviet Jews became despondent after Brezhnev began enforcing more oppression on freedom of expression. The backlash Jews experienced for Zionist demonstrations that were inspired by Israel at the time manifested itself in an increase of anti-Semitic propaganda that compared Israel with Hitler's Nazis. Orleck says, "Energetic government enforcement of educational and occupational quotas . . . forced even successful and assimilated Soviet Jews to question what would become of their children if they remained in the Soviet Union."

But assimilation is unfair, and it is an unrealistic expectation to assume that people must alter their entire culture and history in order to live among others. "Throughout history, it's easy to unite people in difficult times against a common enemy," says Andrei. "Jews are always easy targets because they never assimilate. We maintain our identity."

It was this desire to maintain their identity, yet protect Andrei from unnecessary prejudice and potential danger, that caused his father and mother to give Andrei his mother's last name. Victor Treyvas is Andrei's maternal grandfather. Treyvas is a Jewish name, but in Russia it is not as apparently Jewish as Bregman, his father's name.

"It would endanger Andrei in Soviet Russia to give him the last name of Bregman," Victor and his wife urged Andrei's father, and he agreed. So Andrei's last name became Treyvas from his mother's side.

For ten years after the decision was made, Andrei's father's side of the family chose not to talk to them because they did not give Andrei the Bregman name. Their decision to miss out on the early years of Andrei's life resulted in an irreparable estrangement that still exists, but Andrei, his brother and parents, and his maternal grandparents remain very close even now.

But their concerns were valid. Even when Lena, although she was a Treyvas, would write down "Bregman" because it was her married name, she had difficulty getting work. She would be denied employment whenever she used the name "Bregman." As a teacher, even in the universities, it was not the official reason she didn't get hired, but everyone knew that they would take very few Jews. However, since Andrei's parents and grandparents decided to protect him in this way (and his brother, who would be born ten years later), his father's family could never forgive that their name would not go to their grandchildren.

"My father's family were not really very intelligent people," Andrei remembers. "And when my father's mother died, Grandfather married her sister." Andrei's father was twelve when his own mother died, so Andrei never knew his actual paternal grandmother. Andrei's father was raised, then, by his father and his aunt, whom he actually called Mother.

Andrei's grandfather and his new bride had their own child, and so Andrei's father and his sister from their mother were less favored than the new child. Andrei feels that this situation could have been the genesis of the estrangement, and that when the naming situation came up, it gave them an excuse not to be close with Andrei's immediate family. Eventually, when they started talking again, it was still awkward, and Andrei saw them only two to three times each year.

"The funny thing is that I looked very much like the Bregmans," says Andrei. "I look exactly like my father's father." Andrei doesn't look like his mother's father, because Victor has more of a Slavic look from his Russian mother. Victor is blond and has green eyes, and Andrei got the Jewish looks. "The irony is that, when I would be there and all the relatives would be there, he would sit with his grandson from his second marriage, who looked more like his wife's side of the family," says Andrei. "I looked just like him, and we were not close." Someone in the family would say, "Oh my God, Andrei, you look just like him!" However, he and Andrei were so estranged that Andrei didn't even call him Grandfather. He called him Mr. Bregman.

In fact, as with many languages, in Russian there are two different forms of the word "you." One form is for someone you know well, and the other is a more formal one that you use for people you do not know well. Andrei always referred to Mr. Bregman in the formal version.

Andrei's great-grandmother was the only Christian in the family. She was a Russian woman who was a nurse before the Revolution. After the First World War, during the Revolution, she met a doctor. At this time, the Russian White Army was fighting the Russian Red Army. She married the doctor, who happened to be a Jew. She believed in God and went to church regularly, which was very dangerous back then, because Communist Russia was an atheist state. Russia was a very atheist country. It was mandated so. But she went anyway, being very dedicated to her faith and to the Russian Orthodox Church. She even held a high position within the Church. And although Andrei never thought of himself as Christian or Russian—always Jewish—he still has his great-grandmother's cross.

In fact, Jewish was not necessarily a spirituality for Andrei, but more of a nationality. And he has always identified himself as being Jewish rather than Russian. The rest of his family are all Jewish. "Regardless if you were practicing or not, you were either Jewish-Russian, Russian, or Ukranian, and that was always marked in your passport," says Andrei.

In America, people who are born here are American citizens. However, those born in Russia were considered citizens, but they would specify the nationality of every person. This was an anti-Semitic tactic that Russia used until 1992 that is similar to the "separate but equal" ideology fiasco in America.

Andrei's nationality was Jewish. To Andrei, it is important that people don't confuse the Jewish nationality with the religion, partly because he never remembers his father going to synagogue.

Andrei's Jewish identity wasn't a factor until he started

going to school, where every class had a journal that also stated each student's nationality. As with the passports, it would either specify that a student was Russian, Ukranian, or Jewish. Of the forty students in Andrei's class, approximately thirty of them were Russian, six were Jewish, and the remaining four would be Ukranian or another nationality.

So the anti-Semitism the Soviet Jews experienced was not based on religion, even though Russia was an atheist country. In fact, religion didn't really exist in Russia. But Andrei always knew he was Jewish because of the nationalistic anti-Semitism. When a person was Jewish, everyone knew it.

All the passports in Andrei's family said "Jewish" except, of course, for his great-grandmother's, which is why his mother was never able to get a very good teaching job. However, Andrei's grandfather Victor had a choice because his mother was Russian. He chose to put "Russian" on his passport, which enabled him to have a great job. He was respected and was making most of the money for the family, allowing them to live very comfortably.

When Andrei was born, his mother kept working, and his grandmother left music school to be with him. Despite the estrangement of his father's side of the family and the anti-Semitism of Russia, Andrei began his life under the umbrella of his closely knit extended family who loved him very much. It was this very environment in which the sexuality of a future porn star began to emerge.

2

It was late when four-year-old Andrei awoke. It could have been the summer sun filtering through the curtains of his family's country house that finally stirred him. It could have been the sound of his grandmother downstairs, or the smell of the *kasha* or sandwiches she was making for breakfast. It could have been the sound of other children playing outside, or perhaps just the natural end to a perfect night's sleep. Andrei loved to sleep at the country house.

In the fall, Andrei spent every weekend at the country house with his grandfather, Victor, and helped him work in the garden. In the spring, Andrei's father would join them on their weekends away from the hustle and bustle of busy Moscow to work in the garden and to prepare the house for the summer. Then, Andrei's mother and grandmother would start going with them when it got warm, and they would all spend the summer there. Each day of the summer, Andrei's parents and his grandfather drove or took the train into Moscow for work, leaving Andrei with his grandmother in the huge country house.

The house was so big that four families could easily occupy the house's two floors at the same time. So the five of them (and later, the six of them) were extremely comfortable there. Just like Andrei, his mother Lena had also spent her childhood growing up at the country house, and had a lifelong friend who lived nearby. Andrei had become very good friends with the daughter of his mother's friend.

Of course, at four years old, and even later as the two of them grew up, there was nothing sexual between them. They were just friends, and they played together every day. She and Andrei went swimming during the day, or hiked in the forest and looked for mushrooms.

Even though Russia was Communist, a class system still existed among its citizens. Victor, Andrei's grandfather, was a high-ranking engineer since he was able to put "Russian" as his nationality on his passport. Victor's wife was a piano teacher. Andrei's father was also an engineer, and his mother was a literature teacher. This middle-class life is how it was possible for Andrei and his family to have an apartment in Moscow, and the country house, which was located about an hour outside the city.

Although the class system existed to some degree in Russia, it was not the same way Americans perceive it. There was no such thing as a literal "middle class," but Andrei's family—largely because of his grandfather's job—was considered more upper-level. For example, the Treyvas family owned a car, and not many people could have a car.

The country house had been inherited from Victor's parents, who had bought the house, making Andrei the fourth generation in the family to have the comfort of the country house.

As Andrei grew up, he got more friends in addition to the daughter of his mother's friend. Eventually, his circle included about ten children, both boys and girls of varying but close ages, who would go to the beach every day of the summer. Andrei and his group would stay out in the sun from about noon until four or five o'clock in the afternoon. After dinner, they played games.

"We didn't play in ways that you think of in America," Andrei recalls. "There were never any organized things like basketball or football." Instead, in the evening, Andrei and his friends would all be somewhere in the forest near the country house; they would have a fire and bake potatoes. If the weather permitted, the group would return to the beach at the lake.

Boats of all kinds sailed and motored by across the lake in the beautiful dusk with laughter and shouts of repartée and frolic trailing along. The smell of the water and the spray of the mist from the lake served to cool things off at the close of the day, while crowds of friends like Andrei's enjoyed the sand and sunset.

In addition to groups of friends, many children went to the beach with their parents. However, Andrei's parents did not like the beach as he did. When Andrei was younger, he went with the parents of his friends. Eventually, the group went on its own.

Lena particularly did not like the beach. While she wasn't a large woman, she also wasn't skinny, and felt self-conscious about other people seeing her in her bathing suit. In Andrei's family, ironically, nobody would take his or her clothes off in public. In Russia, it is customary for people to go to the steam room, but the Treyvas family would never do it. They weren't exactly Puritans, but there was no such thing as nudity among Andrei's family.

Andrei was shocked one day when he saw a friend's mother change clothes in front of him. Even though the woman wasn't naked, as she was still wearing a bra when she changed her top, Andrei was surprised by the way she didn't seem to give a thought to the children seeing her change clothes. His mother would never have changed clothes in front of him where he could see her bra, nor would he ever have had the occasion to see his father's underwear. It simply was not done.

"I know that my father has a huge dick, just because you can see," says Andrei. "But it was never purposely shown or seen because he never changed in front of me." Andrei's parents just did not feel it was necessary to change in front of their children.

The product of strict Russian mores, Andrei's family did not know how to handle the sexuality that seemed to be burgeoning in their son at the early age of four. In the area around their country house in the summer of 1976, there were approximately twenty to twenty-five children. Problems began for Andrei at this time because he was already starting to feel curious about sexuality.

During sleeping hour, when the children would be napping, Andrei began messing around with the other children, boys and girls, whoever would be next to him. "I remember two guys very well," Andrei says. "And there was one girl. I would touch their genitals, and they would touch mine." There was one boy in particular whom Andrei liked very much, and the two of them touched each other frequently.

Often children at this age become curious about the genitals of other boys and girls, and bouts of I'll-show-you-mine-if-you-show-me-yours commonly tend to result. Some touching even occurs on a relatively frequent basis. But in Communist Russia, no information existed that would help adults deal with the situation in a way that would be healthy for the children. Even in America, boys are jokingly told that masturbation will make them go blind, or that it will cause hair to grow on their palms. In Russia, it went beyond this sort of deterrent.

Eventually, the caretaker complained to Andrei's mother.

When she arrived, Andrei was sitting on the floor, and she confronted him about it immediately.

"Is it true?" Lena asked. "What's going on?"

"No," Andrei lied. Embarrassed by his actions, and not knowing why he should be, Andrei continued playing with his toys and jumping around as if to ignore the situation.

"Andrei," Lena said, pressing her son for the information she did not want to hear. "If you tell me the truth now, we will all respect you and think that you are the most honest person in our family."

"Yes," Andrei said. Naively, he believed her and admitted to touching the children, and letting them touch him. "I did it."

When they got back to the country house, Andrei was confined to his room, unable to go out for hours. When Victor came to talk to Andrei, he got more afraid of the situation. In fact, the whole family was afraid of Victor—Andrei's grandfather—the patriarch of the family. Victor was in charge of hundreds of subordinates at work, and he had an element to him that made him sort of a tyrant. So Andrei was incredibly afraid of how his grandfather would react.

Even though Victor had never hit Andrei, and never would, Andrei was very scared. It is important to realize that this was a house full of Russian Jews. There was a lot of love in the house, but conflict was dealt with through raised voices. "You can't come back to the country house for two weeks," Victor said. It was a punishment that devastated Andrei because he didn't understand what the problem was. He hadn't done anything. They were just touching each other. They were only four years old.

It would be another thirteen years before Andrei would do anything else with anyone. But this situation made his parents constantly afraid, as Andrei was growing up, that he was touching his penis. Although he was touching it, he was never masturbating, which Andrei now understands is what they were afraid he was doing. Russia of the 1970s and 1980s was similar to the United States of the 1930s and 1940s as depicted in the film *Kinsey*, until Professor Kinsey came along and did his study. Except Russia did not have Alfred Kinsey. In fact, there was no sexual knowledge allowed at all.

Andrei's parents and grandparents thought that it was very dangerous for children to masturbate. Whenever his hands would be in his pockets, they would yell at him right away and tell him to take them out. "Why can't I leave them there?" Andrei asked, genuinely confused.

They told Andrei that his lips would hang and that saliva would drip down, and that it was very dangerous, that he should never touch himself there. But they were simply afraid that he was masturbating. He was also never allowed to have his hands under the covers when he was in bed. In fact, he was already getting erections and touching his penis when they weren't looking, but he wasn't masturbating yet.

Andrei's parents and grandparents were not operating out of malice. They, too, were uninformed about the sexual development of children and teenagers. It was because nothing was available to them in the way of information. Clearly, ignorance is not bliss. Keeping information away from citizens as a result of a political agenda is damaging and counterproductive in any society. And this lack of information would come back to haunt Andrei when puberty arrived and the threat of masturbation became real.

3

Just a year or two after Andrei began school, his great-grandmother, the only Christian in his family, passed away. This changed the dynamic of his family in a profound way. His great-grandmother had been living in a two-room apartment of her own, what would be the American equivalent of a one-bedroom. Until she died, Andrei and his parents had lived all together with his grandparents. In Russia it was common for everybody to live together in a small apartment. However, Great-grandmother's apartment was in a good area, so it gave them the opportunity to get out on their own, and he and his parents moved into the apartment she had been living in.

Although this was a dramatic change from the way things had been, the apartment was only half an hour away on foot, or ten minutes by cab. And every day, Andrei's grandmother would pick him up after school and take him home. She would then stay with him until his mother returned from teaching. Another thing that gave Andrei continuity during this period of adjustment was the country house. He continued going there every weekend with his grandfather in the fall and spring, and he looked forward to the summers when the whole family would be there all the time.

In addition to the change at home, the move meant that Andrei would be going to a new school. But the change in schools in the second grade introduced Andrei to a girl who would be one of his closest friends throughout his life. Her name was Ivanna.

Ivanna felt that Andrei was always sweet and bright, even brilliant. Upon meeting him, she recognized that he was interesting and somewhat an outcast. A bit of an outcast herself, she was drawn to Andrei, and the two of them became friends relatively soon after Andrei got to her school.

By the time Andrei was nine, and he and Ivanna had known each other a couple of years, the two of them had become increasingly close. This is the time in children's lives when crushes begin forming. But in school, Andrei and Ivanna were just friends. Andrei was always in love with her, but she never gave him a sign of anything physical.

But the two of them were always together. They went everywhere together, saw movies, and talked on the telephone twice a day, every day. Andrei was still very shy. Neither of them had reached puberty yet, but they were as close as any two nine-year-olds could be.

Andrei reached the onset of puberty a few years later, faced once again with the lack of information that had caused such a misunderstanding when he was touching the other children at the age of four. When Andrei was ten, his brother was born. Until then, he thought babies came from a pill that women got from the doctor.

So, when he and Ivanna reached twelve or thirteen, and things began changing, the ignorance they both faced made adolescence incredibly difficult. But it was particularly difficult for Andrei. Everything was suppressed. They did not know and were not told anything about sexuality. There was no information on straight sexuality, not to mention gay sexuality. "Everything was a disaster, basically," Andrei says. "Growing up in terms of sex."

So without being able to talk to each other about the physical and hormonal changes they were both facing, Andrei and Ivanna focused on other things. They had a lot of fun together and began getting into trouble—not criminal trouble, just teen angst trouble. However, in Russia, teen angst didn't necessarily revolve around sex, drugs, and rock and roll.

It was the 1980s, and the Soviet Union was nearing its end. But Andrei and Ivanna were both Jewish and had been growing up in Communist Russia their whole lives. It was prohibited to exercise one's right to the Jewish religion. Going to synagogue could be extremely dangerous. Even though their parents were against it, the two of them rebelled and went anyway, despite the threat of serious consequences for both of their families.

Andrei and Ivanna found the only synagogue in Moscow, which at the time was a happening place. All the young Jewish people went, so it was a place to meet other people. Once again, although Andrei identified himself as a Jew, in his family the traditions were never kept. Although they never celebrated high holidays, it was during a high holiday when he and Ivanna first went to synagogue together. They went with the families of other Jewish friends who did keep the traditions. "But still," says Andrei, "to be Jewish in Russia back then had nothing to do with religious traditions much." At least it didn't for Andrei.

Even with good friends, plenty to do, and no information about sexuality, a young, sexually curious gay boy getting rushes of pubescent hormones on a regular basis will be distracted by the goings-on in his Communist Russian pants. And Andrei was coming very close to getting the shock of his life.

4

At the age of fourteen, Andrei discovered masturbation, but not in the way most boys in America discover it, through curiosity and self-exploration. Andrei had been experiencing erections for years, but had consistently been deterred from touching himself in any way.

One day while lying in the bathtub, a stream of water shot up the length of Andrei's penis, causing him to reach orgasm spontaneously. When the sperm shot out of his penis, he became terrified and thought he was dying. Lying in the tub, covered in bath water, Andrei experienced turmoil. With every spasm and twitch of his erection that was producing more and more of this thick, white discharge, he could only imagine that something was terribly wrong.

In a mixture of hormones, fear, and ecstasy, Andrei's terrible experience finally came to an end. Afterward, when he realized he wasn't going to die, he allowed himself to understand that it actually had felt good, whatever it was that had happened. However, he knew he couldn't tell anyone, for fear of a reaction like he had gotten at the country house when he and the other children had messed around.

For months and months, the situation was a huge trouble for Andrei because he kept wanting to do it every time he took a bath or shower. After a few months, he figured out that he could get the same thing to happen without being in the shower, without the stream of water, and Andrei discovered the pleasures of masturbation.

This is a defining example of the oppression of Soviet Russia and one of the consequences of withholding health information. No men in Russia had any sexual information. Across the board, gay or straight, there was nothing to guide them. Men didn't even talk to each other about it. In America, men are constantly comparing and competing with each other regarding their sexual exploits.

But the oppression of Communism resulted in trauma and confusion for Andrei. "It's so disgusting, and it traumatized people very much," Andrei says of the strict environment. "I was very much traumatized by it, and by those sexual experiences and even with masturbation. It's really disgusting that I suffered for no reason."

Andrei told himself over and over that if he didn't stop masturbating, there would be horrible consequences, and he had no one to turn to that he could talk to about it. The worst thing about it was that Andrei was discovering that he was attracted to men, giving him another feeling of isolation that struck at his core. He felt as if he were completely alone in the world.

When he didn't think things could get any worse, his feelings of loneliness were soon replaced by feelings of fear. He eventually realized that other homosexuals existed by hearing reports about them going to jail. So for young gay men growing up in Communist countries, there is absolutely nothing that could validate the feelings they develop. In America, it is bad enough that the government creates damaging propaganda and discourse against its own gay/lesbian/bisexual/transgendered (GLBT) citizens. However, at least in America, there are people who work very hard to combat the "trickle-down" hatred perpetuated by those elected to represent the public. GLBT youth like Andrei, growing up in Communism, didn't even have that.

Like many GLBT youth, Andrei had girlfriends. But he knew deep down that they were only serving to cover his true sexuality. This is what he chose instead of scorn and possible legal consequences. But he knew he wanted to be with a guy, and he found it incredibly disturbing.

Andrei began to develop signs of depression. He continued to masturbate, but he also continued to beat himself up about it. Once he learned he could do it outside the shower or bath, the frequency with which he did it increased to no less than twice a day, every day. Every time, he felt as if he were damaging himself in some way.

The film *Kinsey* shows how American teens were going through the same thing in the thirties, forties, and fifties. Masturbation was considered dangerous not only morally but medically as well. As a teen, Andrei once found a brochure for teenagers that said it was very bad to masturbate. "It didn't explain why, but I remember it saying it was terrible," Andrei says. "Which made me more afraid. I would never talk to anyone about those things. We never had classes in school. Those things were never discussed. We were left on our own."

In addition to the problems Andrei was having on his own with masturbation, he was also having trouble at school. Andrei and Ivanna had to deal with all kinds of people on a daily basis. Many people didn't like either of them, which was actually one of the aspects that brought the two of them closer together. The students gave Andrei a hard time for not being butch enough. But the teachers and administrators, many of whom had grown up in the Stalin era, did not like free-spirited people like Andrei and Ivanna. So the two friends clashed with those kinds of people a lot.

Eventually, Andrei started acting out. In his school, a

student would get chosen to be a sort of leader. This student wore a red cloth to indicate this leadership, similar to a hall monitor, or even a classroom monitor. When Andrei painted an American flag on the red cloth, the administrators at his school considered it the last straw.

"It was a great, great sorrow for me," says his mother, Lena. "I cried. Because the teacher was awful. She was awful, and she hated him. His manner was a little feminine, with more gestures and movements than normal. And she laughed at him, and she wanted the other pupils to laugh. She was very unfair. And it was clear to me that she was not honest. At first I came and tried to argue with her, and I wanted her to understand that she's not right. And I saw that she didn't want to be honest. She had her aim, and her aim was to treat him badly.

"At first, I was afraid of her because a teacher was a great power at school at that time. She was like Stalin—a very Stalin-ish woman. When I understood that she was a bad woman, I started to tell her what I really thought about her. And I took him from that school. The school studied English heavily, and I didn't want to take him from there, but I had to. But it was for the best."

Even though Andrei had to leave the school and start attending elsewhere, the six years of friendship he and Ivanna had built were not going to be dissolved by geography. They had already formed the basis for a friendship that would endure forever for the both of them. They would no longer be going to school together, but they would eventually come to lean on each other in ways that neither of them expected or imagined.

At his new school, Andrei met a new friend, Anna. The way she met him when he came to her school was very similar to the way Ivanna had met him six years earlier. Neither of the two were popular in school, and Anna knew right away that Andrei was not like the other boys.

"From the beginning, he was different," says Anna. "He was smart. He was very interested in books, art, and the theater."

In addition to his interest in the arts, Anna knew that Andrei was very interested in clothes. Clothes were difficult to come by in Russia at the time, but Andrei always found a way to get what he wanted. Russia had a deficiency in everything, but an example of the way clothing was hard to come by can be seen in Russian movies of the time period. Actresses in Russia sometimes wear the same dress in as many as four movies. A lot of Russian women had between one and three dresses total, and wore them for years. It was very different from American capitalist culture.

Andrei's interest in clothes and his ability to get things he wanted resulted in massive jealousy among his peers. In addition, male ego was a big thing in Russia. Because he was interested in the arts and he dressed as well as he could, the other boys would taunt him and call him gay. Even if it's true—sometimes especially if it's true—hateful taunts about who you are can do permanent damage. His only way to combat the taunts was to have a girlfriend, whom he kept throughout high school.

Andrei began to realize in high school that he did not belong in Russia. The administrators and teachers at his new school were not like the barbarians at his previous school. However, taunts from the other children that were rooted in hatred toward something Andrei knew was inherent, in addition to the way he was seeing Jews and homosexuals being treated by the government, were clear signals that a better life existed somewhere else for him. Through films, news, and anti-Western propaganda, Andrei began to feel the call of the land of opportunity.

5

Being gay in Russia in the 1980s, Andrei had no one to talk to. Andrei was getting more and more isolated and upset because he knew that he was attracted to guys, but had to keep up appearances by having a girlfriend throughout high school. In addition to keeping up appearances, Andrei thought that having a girlfriend could "cure" him of being gay. Later, when his girlfriend emigrated to Europe, and Andrei went to university, he would give in and start having sex with guys.

But during his last couple of years at high school, Andrei began hearing that in the West, being gay was actually considered normal. Although a positive public opinion toward gays in the United States is taking a long time to develop, the American Psychological Association (APA) stopped considering homosexuality a sickness in 1974. Since then, the APA has been proactive about discussing the benefits of sexual health that result from understanding and embracing all sexual and gender identities.

Once Andrei learned that homosexuality was normal in the West, he wanted nothing more than to leave Russia. In addition, he began to make peace with himself and made up his mind that he would no longer attempt to change his sexual orientation.

Andrei never made a big coming-out presentation to his mother, but combined discussions related to homosexuality that she had with him made it clear to her that he was leaning in that direction. Throughout high school, she tried to talk him out of it, not only because she was afraid for his safety, but at the time she didn't think it was the right way to live or be. Once Andrei made peace with himself about it, he would begin making it clear to her that it wasn't going to change.

It was because Andrei viewed the West as a place where he could be gay that he began to idealize the West very much. Being gay was not just normal there, but it was a good thing; it was acceptable. Andrei didn't know about the civil rights fight GLBT people were going through in the 1970s and 1980s after the Stonewall Inn riots of 1969. He didn't know about all the problems and discrimination. From the time he was fifteen years old, Andrei's thoughts were toward the West. He knew he wanted to live in America.

Part of the reason the GLBT civil rights struggle didn't make it to Russia was because of its anti-West movies. The films would depict homosexuals in a bad light if they wanted to portray someone who was evil. This kind of attack hits hard when you realize that's what you are. So, Andrei reframed those depictions into making them mean that he should be excited that there were so many people like him in the world. The films were showing that in the West, being gay was considered a good thing; they were showing that the West was immoral. But for Andrei, it was vindication.

Andrei's self-image was forming under this oppression, and eventually he would come to realize that people liked how he looked. "It's strange to live in a society that oppresses you so much," Andrei says. "Then you find out that you're actually good-looking and that it's okay to take your clothes off." Andrei was adorable as a child, by all accounts, but felt like he went through an awkward phase from the time he was five until he went to university. "I was not a good-looking teenager," he says. "I had huge lips and white skin, and I was not popular in school. I was not a cool guy." Andrei says he never felt sexy or sexual, or beautiful, when he was growing up.

So, in addition to his struggles with sexuality, he had the added suffering of going through life thinking he was ugly, always wanting to be beautiful and popular. As Andrei grew into his looks and started to realize he actually *did* look good, he was incredibly happy to have them because he didn't feel spoiled by them. To him, his attractiveness was brand new.

"Is it true that people say I'm good-looking?" he asked his mother one day, because he didn't believe it at first. Once he turned sixteen, however, people were definitely starting to take notice.

"You know, Andrei," she said. "You don't have to worry about anything. Your father is a very good-looking man." She explained to Andrei that he was always destined to be an attractive man. Being an optimist, and wanting it so badly after years of feeling inferior, Andrei allowed himself to believe her.

It didn't matter to Anna whether Andrei was an ugly duckling or a swan, because that wasn't the nature of their friendship. They continued to be best friends, just as Andrei had been with Ivanna. In fact, their friendship grew as the years went by. As with clothing, Russia was deficient in theater, making it difficult to get tickets on a regular basis. However, Andrei could always get tickets so that he and Anna had something to do.

Often, the Russian mob was the source of the tickets.

Once when the men started throwing sexual innuendo in Andrei's direction in relation to the tickets, Andrei (still feeling insecure about his sexuality as a Russian Jew) telephoned his father and had him meet the two of them outside the theater after the show. Andrei was willing to get the tickets he wanted, but refused to be intimidated for it, even as a teenager.

Other times were less dramatic. Sometimes, he stopped people at the door, asking if they had extra tickets. Being very persuasive and coming into his good looks, if Andrei wanted something, he always got it. "He always knew about movies and the theater," Anna says. "So it was always interesting to talk to him."

If something interested him, he knew how to obtain it. It wasn't always easy, but he did whatever he needed to do, and still does. It wasn't about money in Russia at that time; it was about connections. He got what he wanted, but he didn't want much.

In addition to the theater, whether they were showing films, plays, opera, or the ballet, Andrei also took Anna to synagogue the way he and Ivanna had gone. Again, Russia didn't like religion in general. In fact, it didn't like it at all, but synagogue was especially frowned upon because Jewish people were trying to leave Russia at that time. In *Red Blues: Voices from The Last Wave of Russian Immigrants*, edited by Dennis Shasha and Marina Shron, a documentary filmmaker named Aaron Kanevsky recalls, "I was deprived of many freedoms in Russia and I couldn't always do what I wanted. But what a person wants doesn't matter. After all, all of great literature is based on that conflict between the desirable and the possible, the struggle between what you want and what you can do."

So, although Anna was not Jewish as Andrei and Ivanna were, he took her to synagogue in order to share his experience with her. They ended up going regularly. And each time they arrived, secret police were standing nearby, covertly, but there were a lot of them. "It gave you a really strange feeling because you don't know," Anna says. "And I think at that time it was an important part of Andrei's life. It wasn't so much about religion. It was about the Jewish culture and heritage."

This connection with his heritage, the news of many Russian Jews immigrating in the West, and the pressure he felt to leave due to his sexuality, all combined to push Andrei forward. He wanted to go to America, and again it was clear early on that Andrei got what he wanted. For Andrei, the West seemed like a door because he was Jewish and gay. He always wanted a better life, and he realized it would only be possible in the West, because things had started to change in Russia and people (including Andrei) began to have hope.

Andrei's parents and grandparents knew that Russia was not the place for him, and they knew he would one day leave for the West. However, they wanted him to attend university first. So, in 1990, right after he graduated from high school, Andrei went to university and majored in law.

It was when he went to university that Andrei finally felt free enough to begin having relationships with other young men. During his first year at university, Andrei continued going to the beach with his straight friends. Soon, however, he developed a crush on a young man named Jena (pronounced YENA). Andrei was eighteen, Jena was twenty-three, and Andrei hadn't touched anyone else in fourteen years. He certainly hadn't had sex with anyone yet.

Jena was part of Andrei's group of cool Jewish students, young guys from families whose fathers were engineers and doctors. Andrei and Jena became very good friends. Partying on the beach all the time, Andrei got a tan, and was surprised at how good he looked. It boosted his confidence in a way that let him get close to Jena.

All his friends were cruising girls and partying with girls, but Andrei didn't do that because he had no desire for it. In addition, his high school girlfriend was preparing to leave for Germany. So Andrei felt as if he were falling in love with Jena.

Everything changed for Andrei at that point. His hair was very curly, so he got it cut short, and maintained the tan that made him look so good. When he started his second year at university, he became very popular for the first time in his life. Everyone wanted to be friends with Andrei. It was incredible to be good-looking.

Eventually, Andrei told Jena how he felt about him. "I have a crush on you," Andrei said, not knowing what to expect.

"Oh?" Jena said. Although Andrei knew him as part of his straight crowd of friends, the revelation went strangely because Andrei would soon realize that at that point, Jena was probably bisexual to a degree. "I knew you were gay."

"How could you know that?" Andrei asked.

"Just a guess," Jena said. It shouldn't have surprised Andrei that Jena had guessed. He had been teased about being gay all throughout school, way before he entertained the thought of telling anyone. Besides, when you have feelings for someone the way Andrei was starting to feel about Jena, you look at them differently.

The moment remained awkward for both Andrei and Jena, so nothing sexual or even intimate came from it. Andrei's good looks gave him license to become more and more arrogant. A few weeks later, after the shock had worn off about Andrei's coming out to Jena, Andrei's feelings for Jena were finally requited. But by then, the lack of instant gratification, combined with Andrei's increasing arrogance,

changed how both young men had probably pictured the
situation going.

"Do you want to try it?" Jena asked Andrei.

"With you?" Andrei asked, cock-blocking himself with
his own pride. "Never."

Andrei's new whirlwind life kept him very busy, indeed.
His studies and his friends occupied every moment of his
time and attention. When Andrei was twenty, his grandfather from his father's side—Grandfather Bregman—died
of cancer. "I didn't feel anything," Andrei says of his pass-
ing. It was not Andrei's new busy, popular life that made
him numb to his grandfather's death. It was the fact that
this side of his family had emotionally abandoned Andrei
from the very beginning, all because he wasn't given the
Bregman name. They had isolated themselves from him. "I
had no feelings about him at all because I saw him twice a
year," Andrei says. "People ask me why, and it's simple.
You can't miss something that you never had."

The loss Andrei felt at the age of twenty was not to do
with his family, but rather that of his oldest, dearest friend.
Although they had not been school chums since middle
school, Andrei and Ivanna still lived in the same city. They
had kept in touch, shared friends, and remained close. Andrei and Ivanna had never had a romantic connotation to
their friendship, but Ivanna was set to leave Russia for
Germany.

When they said goodbye, Ivanna leaned into Andrei,
placed her hands gently around his face, and intimately
kissed his pouty lips. Andrei's head began spinning. He felt
faint. It would be several years before Andrei would again
feel such an intimate feeling. The vertigo was a brief respite
from the realization that Ivanna, who had been in his corner since they were five years old, was leaving Russia, and
leaving him behind.

Being the family man that Andrei is, he continued to put

all the emotion he had into caring for his immediate family, including his maternal grandparents with whom he was so close. Andrei's lack of emotion for Mr. Bregman is easy to understand considering they had never been a part of each other's lives. However, there would come a time in Andrei's future when a family member close to him would experience a situation that would devastate him.

6

"I've changed my mind," Andrei said to Jena. "I want to try it. I want to have sex with you." Andrei's pride had given way to the relentless stiffness in the crotch of his pants, and of course, his timing couldn't have been worse.

"No," Jena replied. "You've already said no." The back and forth near-misses and bad timing for both Andrei and Jena prevented them from doing anything other than kiss for several months during Andrei's last year at university.

"I've always asked myself why I originally told him no," Andrei says now. However, he understands with complete clarity that it was because of his burgeoning arrogance. After Jena turned him down, Andrei continued asking Jena if he would have sex with him, basically begging him to do it. Their friendship, which had only a few years of history, suffered for Andrei's persistence in the matter.

Pressure from Lena to be straight and confusion over the on-again-off-again situation with Jena turned Andrei's mind to other possibilities, and he occasionally slept with women. "When I found out all about [Andrei being gay]," says Lena, "I wanted to hide it. I wanted him to change. I talked to him about it a lot. Sometimes I would get angry with him. In my mind I thought it was a great shame to be gay. He didn't want to intentionally hurt me, but the truth was very hurtful." The first woman he ever slept with was at university. Galina, a young married woman, was very successful. Her husband was a very good-looking, very successful doctor.

When Andrei first met Galina, they were just good friends. Eventually, she seemed interested in him and started kissing him. Lena, who knew about Andrei's feelings for Jena (and for men in general for that matter), was thrilled to learn about Galina. They hoped that Galina's influence would send Andrei in the hetero direction for good.

Andrei began taking Galina to the country house for sex. "She was great sex," Andrei remembers. "She had her period very organized, so she knew when we could fuck and when I could cum, and it was great sex really." When Andrei's parents knew she would be coming to the country house, they would leave to give them privacy.

"Galina," Lena once asked, "why are you with Andrei? You have a beautiful husband. You're smart." Lena was kidding to a degree, and was hopeful that Andrei would be straight, but knew deep in her heart that Andrei was simply experimenting. At the time, Andrei was considering the possibility that he might be bisexual, but it was his last year at university, and he had already started going to gay clubs.

Eventually, Galina began to get somewhat needy. The neediness progressed into a situation where she had to know where Andrei was at all times. She called him on the telephone every two hours and wrote him letters (which Andrei still keeps). Although they didn't interfere, Andrei's parents also began noticing Galina's erratic and obsessive behavior. "She got very crazy in the end," Andrei says. "She would actually go nuts. And then I just had to end it." Andrei knew that Galina's feelings weren't healthy for either of them, so he simply let her go.

In July 1994, Andrei graduated from Moscow Law Academy and was certified as a lawyer. He hadn't seen Jena in

months. They had been friends the entire time they had
been at university, but the awkward way they both handled their feelings toward each other drove a permanent
wedge between them.

At the start of summer, Andrei went on a cruise with a
girlfriend to Turkey and Greece. On the trip, he became
friends with the woman who was the cruise director. After
the cruise, she asked Andrei to work for her. Andrei knew
her to be somewhat dishonest, even at this early point in
knowing her, but felt that he had enough business savvy to
overshadow that part of her personality. Through the
cruise director and with a little involvement from Jena on
the side, Andrei opened his own tourist company. He and
Jena became friends again.

Andrei's life was going smoothly again, but he still felt
the draw toward the West. Living near the American Embassy, Andrei frequently passed the facility. He often
looked at the Jews who stood in line outside trying to emigrate to America.

In Shasha and Shron's *Red Blues*, a dominatrix named
Julia says, "I left Russia because there was something in
the air then, a sense that a civil war was about to break
out. I had a ten-year-old daughter. So I took off because I
feared for her life. I liked my life in Russia well enough. In
fact, I had a wonderful life there. But I simply believed that
I had to flee Russia, in the same way that Jews ran away
from Germany in 1933."

This was the last wave of Jews to leave Russia, which
had started with Mikhail Gorbachev and Ronald Reagan,
who opened the doors, enabling thousands of Jews to leave.
Andrei had passed the embassy every day for the past four
years while attending university. Now a successful businessman, he continued to see them, and he burned inside with
jealousy. No matter how good things were going in Russia,
Andrei always knew that one day he would go to America.

Andrei and Jena, once again friends (and in some ways business associates), got into their old routine of tennis-balling their feelings for each other. They kissed casually a few times, deeply a few other times. But Andrei was confused—not only about Jena's intentions and motivations—but also about his own sexuality. "I would get very afraid every time he put his hand on my crotch when I was hard," Andrei says. Andrei knew that Jena had become willing to have sex with him again because Andrei's good looks were getting even better. But apart from that, Andrei was now making large amounts of cash. "This was in 1994," Andrei says. "And I was making the equivalent of about $1,000 a day." Money often changes people, particularly young people who have no real experience with it. Andrei got more arrogant.

His arrogance and inexperience led to trouble with the tourist company. The Russian mafia, no longer a threat as molesters of boys in need of theater tickets, became a more prominent threat to Andrei as an adult. Andrei lost everything—his business, his money, his college crush. The person who caused Andrei to lose it all was connected to Jena in some small way, and so Andrei held Jena responsible for his misfortune. Once and for all, Andrei's and Jena's friendship had crumbled under the weight of financial loss and awkward sexuality. But Andrei still considers Jena the first guy he was in love with.

Jena moved on to other pastures, and now lives in Germany with his wife and children.

Andrei would be moving on as well. His time at university was over. He had been certified to practice law, but never pursued it. He had experimented sexually with women and had his heart broken by his first male crush. He had made and lost his first fortune. His eye was on the West, but Mother Russia had one more bittersweet felicity in store for her wayward son.

7

Andrei was down, but not out. He got a job working for a Russian fashion house as a model. There, he met his next love, Sevastian, and worked with him for nearly a year. Sevastian was the gleam in Andrei's eye and the spring in his step through the last part of 1994 and into the beginning of 1995.

Jena and Galina had been significant people in Andrei's life, but it was Sevastian whom Andrei bound himself to emotionally. Although it was the biggest in Moscow, Andrei describes the fashion house as "kitsch." This was Moscow, remember, not Milan, New York, or Paris. So, Moscow trying to do fashion was like McDonald's trying to do *haute cuisine*. It was sort of sweet and sad because they were giving it the old college try, but it just wasn't anything to shout about.

That didn't stop Russian designer Slava Zaitsev, who had a huge building that had been given to him by the government. Back then, Zaitsev was the only designer in Russia. Andrei went to work for him to get close to all the fashion celebrities. He had recently graduated and had lost his tourist business, and had become a pretty hot ticket in Moscow as a fashion party boy.

"So I started to work for him, showing his ugly clothes," Andrei says, his biting honesty respectfully cutting to the quick. "And he introduced me to his new discovery." Sevastian was basically a secretary working in the designer's office. He was a model, too, but mainly pushed paper. "I walked into his office and saw this guy," Andrei says. "I never, ever saw anything like that in my entire life again. He was the most beautiful man I ever met."

Photographs cannot do Sevastian justice. He personified the definitive male beauty. Sevastian was half Russian, half Moldavian, and was actually from Moldavia. Sevastian's body was tall and beautiful. He had piercing, yet kind eyes that looked out from his poetic, tender face as if to cause the Universe itself to breathe a sigh of wonder. The radiance of his smile caused Andrei to smile in return, in spite of himself. Even the tone in his voice resonated through Andrei in a way that moved him to rapture.

Love at first sight.

That is to say, from Andrei's end. The feeling was not mutual. "What I felt, I felt, oh my gosh," Andrei says. "This man is so much more beautiful than I am." It did not matter to Andrei at first that his love for Sevastian was unrequited.

When the two of them would walk down the street, every head would turn. Andrei always felt that the people were looking only at Sevastian, never at him. But it didn't matter. Andrei's love for Sevastian was completely and totally codependent. The line between love and obsession was blurred in the same way that Galina had been so enamored with Andrei.

Although Sevastian did not return Andrei's feelings of love, he did manage to continue hanging out with Andrei. He was using Andrei for his connections, and Andrei had spent a lifetime building a network of connections throughout Moscow. Sevastian was predominantly straight, but an element of bisexuality allowed him to lead Andrei on while he moved up the Moscow social ladder.

In fact, after their first meeting, the two of them became friends and continued to just be friends for some time. In a similar way when Andrei was nervous about his crush on Jena, he would never make the first step to act on his feelings for Sevastian.

Eventually, people started asking questions about the nature of their relationship. The two of them began going to gay bars, where Sevastian would consistently be hit on by numerous gay Russian men. "Oh, it's so annoying," Sevastian said to Andrei, reacting to the attention. "Why don't I tell everyone that you're my boyfriend? Nobody would hit on me then."

"Sure," Andrei said. His obsession with Sevastian led him to agree to the arrangement because, at this point, he would take what he could get. "I think it's a great idea."

Andrei began to feel, however, that Sevastian was doing it for more than a cover to deflect the unwanted and unsolicited attention from other gay men. But he couldn't be sure that it wasn't just wishful thinking—a hopeful, yet destructive symptom of his obsession with Sevastian—so he didn't know how to approach it.

Andrei also felt that Sevastian was insecure. Sevastian knew that he was beautiful, but in many ways he was insecure at the same time. Sevastian was from a very small town and had come to Moscow to find himself. He had grown up insecure, and the residue of it stayed with him into his adulthood. Clearly, beauty isn't everything.

But it's enough. Once, when Sevastian arrived at Andrei's apartment, Andrei began thinking about how to start something. Insecure himself, Andrei was at a loss for what to do. The telephone rang, momentarily ceasing the panicked, frustrated thoughts that swam through Andrei's mind.

"Oh, sure. I can see you," Andrei said into the telephone. The conversation didn't last long, but Andrei's awareness that Sevastian was listening to his side of the conversation kept him talking even after the other person had hung up. "When, tonight? . . . I don't know for sure, but yeah, probably . . . I'll talk to you tonight. Dinner will be great." Andrei hung up the phone and turned to find Sevastian's piercing eyes glaring. "So, what are you doing tonight?" Andrei asked him.

"I don't know," Sevastian said. "You apparently already have plans."

"I don't know if I have plans, but you and I haven't made any plans together." As the two young men walked to the elevator, Andrei could feel the tension coming off Sevastian like the visible ripples of heat that come off asphalt on hot summer days. "Why do you have such a tone in your voice? You seem very upset that I'm making plans, even though you know we hadn't made plans together. Is there something there?" The question had come out on the tail end just as smoothly as if he were asking Sevastian to pass the salt. The elevator doors opened, and they stepped inside. It almost seemed like a did-I-say-that-out-loud moment, but Andrei knew that he had said it and, this time with the hopeful nervousness back in his voice, he continued, "I mean, do you like me?"

The doors closed on the noisy elevator of an old city.

Sevastian took Andrei in his arms. "Of course I do!" he said, and showered Andrei with kisses.

Andrei's head was spinning. Not with thoughts this time. No, this time it was hard-driving emotion, combined with pure ecstasy and the tight grip of Sevastian's arms around him that brought about the vertigo. The first time Andrei had been so swept away by a kiss was when Ivanna had left for Germany. This time, it was on the lips of the man he loved. Andrei was sure he was going to lose consciousness.

From the moment the elevator doors opened and Andrei stepped out into the world, everything had changed. "What was that?" Andrei asked. "I mean, it was amazing!"

"Well," Sevastian said. "This is spring."

And springtime it was. A kiss at the end of March had caused Moscow and all of Russia to bloom around them. And for the next two months, Andrei followed Sevastian everywhere.

Andrei reminded himself of the chickens at the country house outside Moscow. Every summer, Andrei's family would take five or six hens to the country house. If one of the hens would find a fat worm, or if someone would throw a large piece of food down to them and one picked it up, she would never be able to eat the whole thing. But the determined hen would run about with the morsel securely in her beak, and all the other hens would run after her. But she would never be able to eat the large morsel.

This analogy stuck in Andrei's mind. He was the hen who had bitten off more than he could chew, in the sense that it was an illusion that he had his prize. The other hens were gaining on him.

Several rich gay men would appear at the gay clubs in Moscow. "It's a vulgar, disgusting scene," Andrei says. The men would approach him, basically telling him that they wanted his boyfriend, the love of his life, his Sevastian. They even implied they were willing to pay whatever it cost to make it happen. Eventually, the implications ceased, and Andrei could no longer be coy about the situation.

"How much do you want to hook me up with your boyfriend?" asked a man who Andrei describes as a "mutant Russian millionaire."

"You've got to be kidding," Andrei said, standing up in

offense to the suggestion. Andrei turned to Sevastian, who had been sitting nearby, listening to the conversation. "Sevastian, we are going home."

Once outside the club, Sevastian asked, "What was that all about?"

"It's disgusting," Andrei said, and told him the story, filling in the gaps that Sevastian had missed in the noisy club.

Sevastian listened intently, and when Andrei finished, Sevastian asked, "Who is the guy? Is he connected and important?"

The voice inside Andrei's head told him to run. *Run as quickly as you can away from this man and get out of this relationship.* Andrei's feet did not move.

After that, Andrei constantly felt as if he were being electrocuted. All he could think about was that Sevastian would be with him; he was crazy about him. If he hadn't already passed the point of obsession, the "indecent proposal" had pushed him over the line. He could think of nothing except Sevastian, not even himself, and could never relax. Andrei knew at the time, and understands today, that he should never feel this way about someone; that it should never happen to him.

"I should be thinking about myself, my future, my life," Andrei would consciously try to hammer into his brain. He did not want to live for Sevastian, but found himself doing exactly that. It didn't matter how much he loved Sevastian, or how frequent the sex had become; he knew better. Every weekend they went to the country house to make love. The sex they had was mediocre. But how good could man-on-man sex be between a gay man and a straight man?

"We were never fucking, never," Andrei says. "It was all oral sex and amazing kissing. My God, we would kiss for a long time." The intimacy of the kissing developed into a negative familiarity. Over time, Sevastian got used to Andrei and turned emotionally cold. He discovered that he could control Andrei, and perpetuated a mind game that Andrei obsessively joined in on.

Sevastian would be emotionally distant, so Andrei would stop calling him for two or three days. Then Andrei would finally call him, and for the next three or four days, the two of them would be happy. Sevastian would be all Andrei wanted him to be. Then, Sevastian would turn cold again, and the cycle would start all over.

In Russia, there were no gyms for common citizens. They had built the gyms for rich people. Andrei and Sevastian went there, and walked in to find beautiful marble flooring. Celebrities were around every corner, just hanging out, and Sevastian became very sad. "What's up?" Andrei asked him.

"Look how rich people live," Sevastian said. "That's how I want to live."

Andrei knew it was only a matter of time before Sevastian would leave him. Springtime was waning. It was near the end of May. Sevastian wanted a beautiful life, and Andrei knew he would probably be able to get it. But he would not get it with Andrei.

The final weekend in May, Andrei and Sevastian went to the country house one last time, and things were not going well. "Why don't you want to love me? I love you so much," Andrei said. "I do absolutely love you so much."

"It's not possible," Sevastian said, his emotional tap running ice cold. "It's all not possible. You know that."

Andrei proceeded to beg with him, knowing in his heart that it was the wrong thing to do. He also knew that he was wasting his breath. "Please give me another chance. Give *us* another chance," Andrei said. "I'll do whatever you want. I'll do whatever I can possibly do."

Sevastian made love to Andrei one last time, which only

consisted of him sucking Andrei's cock and swallowing the cum before falling to sleep. Andrei, however, did not sleep at all that night. At dawn, Andrei got out of bed and went into the garden to watch the sun rise. It would be his last time at the country house.

Sometime midmorning, with the sun perched high over the country house, Sevastian woke and joined Andrei outside. The two of them strolled quietly to the beach. The girls who had grown up as Andrei's friends were all there. He and Sevastian sat with them for a short time. Then, as if he had been waiting for the perfect moment, or for a prespecified number of minutes to go by, Sevastian said, "Okay, we should go. We should go back to Moscow."

The two of them stood up, and Sevastian took Andrei into his arms. "Everybody was looking," Andrei remembers. "It was a nice picture, you know, me and him together. Really pretty." The magic of the beach near the country house filled Andrei's lungs as he inhaled the memories of the past twenty-three years in this place. For a moment, his mind rekindled the hope that he and Sevastian would ride off into the sunset together.

But it was only for a moment.

Then, Andrei realized it was only another illusion, a dream. And he didn't want to be the hen any longer. The two young men went back to Moscow. They kissed good-bye, and they both went to their own apartments. Andrei put his head in his hands, rubbing hard to try to snap himself back into reality. He wrapped his arms around the front of his chest and rubbed his shoulders and biceps up and down.

"I took myself in my hands," Andrei says. "And I said I wouldn't be able to stay in this country."

PART TWO

Love for Sale

All power is the willingness to accept respon-
sibility.

—Larry Kramer

8

When Gorbachev and Reagan had opened the curtain, it had become easy for Jews in Russia to emigrate. Those who wanted to do so simply had to show their passport indicating that they were Jewish, or bring in their birth certificate. The way Russia had always separated people by nationality, it was easy to prove that someone was Jewish. So at this time, any country would take Russian Jews as refugees.

However, Andrei's parents had wanted him to finish his education at Moscow Law Academy. So no matter how much he had wanted to leave Russia, in respect for his family, he waited. By the time he graduated from university, lost his business, and got his heart broken, the only countries that were accepting Russian Jews as refugees were Israel and Germany.

By 1995, America no longer considered Jews to be in danger in Russia. America considered Russia a democracy, or close enough to it—a place where Jews were no longer being persecuted. So, only the Jews who already had relatives in America were allowed to immigrate.

Andrei did not feel like he was ready to go to Israel at that point. Also, it was farther from Russia than Germany, and Andrei felt more secure about going to a place that was closer to home. Germany was giving refugee status to everyone who was either Jewish or half-Jewish. Everyone who had at least one Jewish parent was granted status. Also, Andrei had been to Germany before, just not on a relatively permanent basis.

A month earlier, Andrei had traveled to Germany with a group of hairdressers who had a competition in Frankfurt. Andrei, still with the fashion house, added a Germany visa to his passport and went as a hair model. Now, he was ready to take his visa and leave for good. A friend of Andrei's worked for a Russian airline, so he called her right away.

"When is the next flight to Germany?" he asked.

"We have one tomorrow," she answered. "It's going to Munich."

"What is Munich like?"

"Munich is very pretty, green, very comfortable, and very secure," she said.

"I'm bringing the money," Andrei said without hesitation. "Get me a ticket."

On May 30, 1995, Andrei's driver came and took him to the airport. The flight was scheduled to leave that afternoon. But it soon became clear that the flight was not going to depart on time. Eventually, the airline announced that there would be a twelve-hour delay on Andrei's flight. The heat had reached 100 degrees and had caused issues with the runway.

"I'm Nikolai," said another man who was waiting for the same flight. "Everyone calls me Kolya."

"Andrei." He changed seats to get closer to the man. Kolya was very attractive, but Andrei didn't really notice. For the next ten hours, the two of them talked at length. Andrei told Kolya all about his relationship with Sevastian, still licking his wounds. In turn, Kolya told Andrei about a relationship he was having with a girl. Kolya was going to Germany to be with her, since they had arranged a marriage of convenience.

Eventually, Andrei and Kolya got seated on the plane to leave for Munich.

"Where are you actually going?" Kolya asked Andrei. "How much money do you have?"

"Two hundred Deutschmarks."

"Well, for that much, you may get a hotel," Kolya said. "But at this time of night, they will not give you a hotel room. That's the way it is in Germany."

"What else can I do?" Andrei asked. "I mean, if I can't get a hotel room, where else should I try?"

"Why don't you stay with us for a few nights?"

Andrei agreed. After ten hours of talking to Kolya, he couldn't see any reason not to accept his generous offer. At two o'clock in the morning, they arrived in Munich. Andrei was grateful for Kolya because, in the middle of the night in a strange place, Andrei would have had nowhere else to go.

They went to the home of Kolya's wife, a black woman who had done him the favor of marriage so that he could get his papers to live in Germany. Andrei hadn't needed to arrange such a deception, because several months earlier, he had applied to the German Embassy as a Jew and was just waiting for his refugee documents, which were supposed to have arrived.

Being a new man in a new place, Andrei did not know much about what to do. Right away, he started going around robbing the clothing stores. It was remarkably easy, because the shops didn't have security tags and beepers at the doors yet. Andrei boldly went into the stores, chose fine clothing, and took the pieces to the dressing room. He would then put the clothes he wore into the shop back on over the stolen merchandise and leave the store.

Once outside the store, he retreated to the bathroom, removed the stolen clothes and put them into a shopping bag, then went to the next store to repeat the process. By the middle of the day, he would have so many things, he would politely ask the salespeople to watch his bags while he "shopped." They graciously agreed. Sometimes, Andrei would buy something small in order to get a bag from the store.

His plan, which he pulled off skillfully, was to send the items to Russia. A friend of his would sell the merchandise to the fashion-starved citizens of the new democracy, then send Andrei the money for the clothes.

However, on his third day in Germany, Andrei entered a store like he had been doing since he had arrived. He left the store with a leather wallet, and was immediately caught by the undercover security. The police arrived, put Andrei in handcuffs, and took him to jail. Twenty other people from Eastern Europe filled the small, dark cell where Andrei was confined. As soon as his eyes adjusted to the darkness, the other inmates slowly began to approach him.

"What did you do to get put in here?" asked one of the men.

"Shoplifting," Andrei said. "I stole a wallet."

"That's hell," said another inmate, as if to commiserate. "In here for a fucking wallet."

"How long have you been in here?" Andrei asked.

A few of the inmates who had gathered all said they had been in this room for a week.

"I have to be here a week?!" Andrei tried not to let his fear show.

"Not always," said the first inmate. "But they have to keep you at least thirty-five hours."

Andrei said to himself that he would rather die than sit in this cell, the stench of twenty men shitting and sweating around him in the dark. He was terrified. However, only twenty minutes after being brought to the cell, the guards brought him his shoelaces and belt. They fined him 150 Deutschmarks and released him.

He went back to Kolya and his wife's house, knowing he could not risk another incarceration. Andrei knew by just that one experience that jail was not a place he could survive. "I need you to help me find a hustler bar," he said to Kolya.

9

I was smart about it. I would not go to anyone's house at night. I was working during the day and in the evening, unless it was something scheduled. I would not be greedy and go twenty-four hours like some escorts. If you're doing this job, you have to remember there are three main rules in how to make it successful.

MICHAEL LUCAS'S THREE RULES OF ESCORTING

RULE 1. Know when to turn your phone off—and have two phones, one for your clients and one for yourself. And always remember, there is a time when you should turn it off. If someone wants you, he will call you again. You should still keep your private life. If you are meeting your friends for dinner, you should leave your work phone off until dinner is over. Otherwise, you will lose all your friends, because no one will be interested if you're always canceling just because a client called.

RULE 2. You should know how to recognize who is on the phone. Never go to someone who's calling you at five o'clock in the morning all stoned. You're asking for trouble. I did it several times; then I stopped doing that, because it's kind of dangerous.

RULE 3. Always be 100% in control—never stoned, never drunk, because then you're not in control. You have to use your head. You don't know with whom you're dealing. You don't trust a person you don't know. You never know who will open the door. Don't ever party with a person, and never drink with a client. My life was easy; I never ran into trouble. I would never even drink their water, because I had heard that sometimes it's possible that they will put something in your water. So I brought my own bottle of water. And because I don't drink, it was easy to not accept any alcohol they offered. I would just tell them I don't drink."

10

"A what?" Kolya asked.

"I need to find a club," Andrei said. "I heard they exist in Germany. Where there are guys where you go and get men and they will pay you money for sex. We should find this bar."

As any good friend would, Kolya readily agreed to help Andrei locate a bar where he could become a male prostitute. At the time, Andrei's English was very bad, and he did not speak German at all. The language barrier made it more difficult than it probably should have been. But the public can be fool-hearted and even menacing to someone looking for such an establishment, inspiring them to send you in the wrong direction.

The situation was embarrassing for both Andrei and Kolya, but they marched on. Their persistence was rewarded when someone finally told them to go to a club called Alexander's. It was approximately five o'clock in the evening when the young men arrived at Alexander's. The Munich bar was small, nicely designed, and full of boys from Eastern Europe. It was common for there to be ten escorts to twenty clients through the week. On weekends, the small bar was packed with twenty boys and one hundred clients. On first impression, it looked lucrative.

Andrei and Kolya had been at the club only five minutes when Alexander, the bar's owner and namesake, approached Andrei. "Someone is asking you what you want to drink," he said kindly.

"Well, I drink water," Andrei said.

"You're a cheap date," Alexander said.

"Well, not really," Andrei said.

"That's none of my business, young man."

Andrei vaguely remembers the man who sent him the drink, but only because he was his first in terms of escorting. Andrei accompanied the man to his place, where he made his first easy 200 Deutschmarks, which is approximately $120—very cheap, as Andrei would soon learn. In spite of the low price, Andrei was paid. It was easy cash, because the only thing the client wanted to do was suck Andrei's cock.

Andrei returned to the bar, and before the evening was over, he had made 600 Deutschmarks. "I'm staying in the West," Andrei told Kolya. He was excited by his prospects, now secure in knowing that he could make it on his own outside the oppression of Russia. "I love this! It's so easy to make money." Andrei ended up staying with Kolya and his wife for nearly a week and a half before moving on.

Every evening, Andrei went to Alexander's, and every evening he would entertain one to three clients. After a week in Germany, Andrei met a young man named Marco. He did not fall in love with Marco, because he was still in love with Sevastian, or at least the illusion of Sevastian. He knew, even looking back, that the reality of his relationship with Sevastian had not even been close to his fantasies of how it should have been.

Marco was a half-German, half–South African man who had been born and raised in Namibia. He'd lived there with his family until he moved to Germany because his grand-mother was German. Marco was immediately fluent in German. It would be much later before Andrei would find out that Marco's family had fled to Namibia from Germany after World War II. Andrei could only assume that it had been because they were Nazis. It was common that many Nazis left Germany for Namibia, Argentina, and other countries abroad. However, Marco had told Andrei that his father was German and his mother was Jewish.

Andrei began saving all the money he was making as an escort. Soon, he purchased medical insurance, which he had made priority one. It was unusual for a man coming from a Communist country to need medical insurance, because health care had always been free for him. But he was prepared that it would be something he would have to pay for. Andrei understood that doing what he was doing would require good health care. And when he eventually came to America, he again would make getting medical insurance his first plan of action.

Eventually, Andrei's refugee papers came through. After escorting at Alexander's for four or five months, Andrei started to travel to different cities. After a weekend in Hamburg, he would return to Munich with several thousand Deutschmarks. Abroad, he would have five or six clients a day, every day. Eventually, Andrei also started traveling to Amsterdam, Switzerland, and all over Europe making money. He expanded his client base when he discovered gay magazines with hustler ads in the back. Back then, the Internet was not yet popular enough for Andrei to be aware of it. Yet he was still making buckets of money from the ads in magazines, which were sold all over Europe, particularly in German-speaking countries like Switzerland.

Before the end of that first year away from Russia, Andrei sought out his first experience with porn. In Germany, he participated in a straight porn film, but hated the experience. He had traveled to France and had found a director who was casting a porn film. The only thing that had inspired Andrei to seek out this new extension of his lucrative career was the simple desire to be exposed to the camera.

Being realistic about his chances in Hollywood, Andrei knew that if he wanted to get into film, he would need to use his strongest assets. He was experiencing so much success in the sex industry already, it seemed like a natural progression. Andrei was aware that anyone's chance in Hollywood is "very little, even if you are gorgeous, and even if you are talented and taking classes, it's a very small chance."

Finding it unfortunate that so many young hopefuls overestimate their chances, Andrei decided early on that he would not wait for the chance to come. He would not wait tables while he hoped for that casting call. He wanted to get as close as he could to a career in film and modeling, and felt that porn was the best way to go. "If the choice would be between porn and legitimate film, of course I would take legitimate film like everybody else," Andrei says. "But you know what? You have to be very realistic. I love what I'm doing, and I'm so very happy that I made the decision when I was young—well, young*er*."

Andrei became friends with many of his clients, many of whom were incredibly rich. They started asking him why he didn't have several guys. The clients convinced Andrei that he could make more money if he were to book a team of escorts out to his clients, and Andrei put together ten guys. One of his best escorts was Kolya, the man who had introduced Andrei to Germany.

Kolya was given Andrei's best clients. One, in particular, was a man named Hans. Kolya and Hans's relationship developed first into friendship; then the two of them became lovers. When Hans died from throat cancer, he left Kolya the equivalent of something close to half a million dollars. "I feel like I did a good thing for Kolya," Andrei says in retrospect. "A nice payback. And for Hans, who was a very nice guy and who always was very good to me."

"I didn't know what he did there [in Europe]. He never told me," says Lena, Andrei's mother. "If I knew everything, maybe I would suffer. I suffered a lot, because we are ordinary people, we are straight. So the world of gay was very, very far from us, and all the people who surrounded us were from the same world. So we didn't want him to differ. But when he was in Germany, we didn't know everything about it.

"But time went on, and we decided that what he does doesn't do harm to anybody. What he wants to do must bring happiness to him. He has to live his own life. And we became accustomed to his life."

With all of Andrei's success in escorting, pimping, and with his first porn film under his belt, he still had a hard time getting over Sevastian. Marco was there, but it simply wasn't the same. It would be several months before Andrei would again feel the rush of emotions that true love brings. In the meantime, there were men to service and escorts to manage.

PART THREE

Michael Lucas—A Star Is Born

Homosexuality strikes at the heart of the organization of Western culture and societies. Because homosexuality, by its nature, is nonreproductive, it posits a sexuality that is justified by pleasure alone.

—Michael Bronski

11

Andrei was simply not happy with Marco. It may have been the fact that he, in no way, could measure up to Sevastian. It may have been the fact that Andrei was still kicking about Europe, when what he really wanted was to go to America. He had wanted to be in America since he was a child. There were a number of factors, but they all culminated into the fact that things were not working out.

Andrei was successful in Germany, but he had been relatively successful when he left Russia as well. Andrei was always going to be successful, no matter where he was or what he was doing. It wasn't about whether or not he was making money. The point was that he was outgrowing Germany altogether, and Marco just happened to be a part of that.

"I was just not happy with Marco," Andrei says. "It was just a done thing, and I wanted to move farther, to America. We were just kids, and he was not what I needed." Marco was too simple for Andrei. Andrei had gone from one extreme, which was Sevastian who wanted more than Andrei could give him, to the other extreme, which was Marco who was content with the status quo that had been established soon after Andrei had arrived in Germany.

Andrei needed a partner who could stimulate him intellectually. By the beginning of 1997, Andrei had turned his mind toward America in a way that had him wanting a man who spoke perfect English. Andrei was itching to make his big move. He and Marco planned a trip to America similar to the trips Andrei had been on to Switzerland. It was to be a working trip, and Andrei had booked himself into a New York club as a stripper. In this club, the man first comes out and dances with his clothes on. Then he goes backstage, and when he returns, he is naked and dancing with a hard-on.

Andrei danced and stripped in the club, then escorted with clients he met there after the shows. After two weeks, Marco went back to Germany. Andrei, who was making good money, decided to stay two more weeks. The writing was on the wall.

At the club, Andrei met a photographer named Charles who wanted to photograph him for a magazine. Andrei readily agreed, particularly since it was in the back of his mind that he wanted to make America his permanent home. This was a way to promote himself in the States. The photographer made Andrei a proposition to do the photo shoot with another man.

"This is Isaiah Remington," Charles said, showing Andrei a picture of Isaiah. "Do you want to do a shoot with this guy?"

"Absolutely!" Andrei said. Isaiah was gorgeous, with blond hair and blue eyes. Very California beach boy. The prospect of doing a photo shoot with him interested Andrei a great deal.

Isaiah had made it clear to Charles that he didn't want to be paid for the photo shoot. He just decided he wanted to be on the cover of a magazine. Isaiah was a clothing merchandiser who had just turned twenty-five. Charles spoke to Isaiah after Andrei had agreed to participate in the shoot and convinced Isaiah to do the same.

On the day of the shoot, Andrei waited with the editor of the magazine, his assistant, and Charles, the photographer. Isaiah, running a little late, was the last one to arrive for the shoot. Andrei liked him from the moment he walked in the door. Perhaps it was the timing, or maybe it was because Andrei was so comfortable in the American setting. But for the first time since Sevastian, Andrei was feeling emotions he had never felt with Marco. For the second time in his life, Andrei was experiencing love at first sight.

"I'm nervous," Isaiah confessed to Andrei. "I really wanted to do this, but I don't know if I can go through with it."

"Just relax," Andrei said as he and Isaiah stripped off their clothes. Once they were down to their underwear, they both sat on the bed. Andrei was concerned for Isaiah and wanted to make him feel better. Andrei moved to get comfortable, and when he did, his foot brushed against Isaiah's foot.

Their first touch sent vibrations through both of them. Their eyes met, Isaiah's full of tension, Andrei's full of lust and sexual energy. Experiencing a rush of confidence like he had never felt before, Andrei pushed Isaiah backward onto the bed and started passionately making out with him. Flashes began bursting as the photographer documented every grope, lick, and kiss.

Isaiah, still nervous after a round of photographs had already been shot, asked to speak to Charles in private before he shot the next roll of film. "All these people here are making me nervous," Isaiah said.

"It's okay," Charles said. "It's just the editor. He's okay."

"No," Isaiah said, politely but firmly. "If they're here, I'm not going to be able to keep my dick hard. I think if there are fewer people here, I'll be able to get hard in between shots."

Reluctantly, Charles stated Isaiah's case to the editor, who finally agreed that he and his assistant would leave. "Hey, listen," Andrei said to Isaiah once they were alone with the photographer. "Why don't you just relax. It's fine. Who gives a fuck?"

"I know," Isaiah agreed. "Now that they're gone, I think it'll be fine."

"Why don't we go for dinner after the shoot?" Andrei suggested.

"Really?"

"Sure," Andrei said in a comforting way. "We'll go for dinner when this is over, and we'll have a great time." It worked. Isaiah loosened up, and the rest of the day went very well. It was Andrei's first photo shoot for an American magazine and his first date with an American man.

When the photographs were first developed, Andrei met with Charles to see them. The photographs showed Andrei kissing Isaiah—finally falling in love again. However, his dinner date with Isaiah after the photo shoot didn't necessarily go as he had imagined it. Isaiah had already made plans with two girlfriends, which he decided to keep and just take Andrei along.

But after the dinner, Andrei went home with Isaiah. They had sex for real this time. No cameras were flashing. No editors were there to kill the mood. Andrei fell quickly in love with Isaiah the same destructive way he had with Sevastian. But Isaiah already seemed much different from Sevastian.

He was everything Andrei had been wanting in a man, and their connection was strong from the very start. As a clothing merchandiser, Isaiah was both creative and intellectual, an irresistible balance for Andrei. Originally from Atlanta, Georgia, Isaiah had grown up in the deep South,

steeped in American traditions foreign even to New York-
ers, so Andrei found him sophisticated in ways that neither Sevastian nor Marco had ever been.

At the same time, however, Isaiah was like Andrei in
that his family ties were strong. His large family included
four beautiful sisters, three of whom were married with
children of their own. The rest of his family still lived in
Atlanta. His youngest sister, still in college, had moved
back home with their father after their mother had died.

The next day, Andrei had to leave. He wasn't going back
to Munich yet; he had gotten a part in an American porn
film and was scheduled to fly to San Francisco to shoot the
film. He and Isaiah said their goodbyes, but both of them
knew they would be seeing each other again. Andrei was
so taken by Isaiah, he was already starting to think about
ways he could leave Germany and come to America per-
manently.

With Isaiah and America on his mind, Andrei boarded
the plane. Andrei already had so much to consider, he didn't
realize he was going to a place that would forever change
a big part of him.

12

Andrei arrived in San Francisco and met with John Rutherford from Falcon Studios. John Rutherford was with Falcon for a total of fifteen years. He was president of the company the last five years he was there. He left Falcon when he had the opportunity to buy COLT Studio Group, another gay porn company that had been started in 1967.

In 1997, however, John Rutherford would be directing Andrei in his first American gay porn film for Falcon. But Andrei's first American film was not the only milestone he would reach with John at Falcon. "We knew he was from Russia, via France," recalls John. Although Andrei had spent most of the previous two years in Germany, he had also spent some of that time in France as well, and that connection to France would eventually result in how Falcon named Andrei. "But coming to us at Falcon, we tried to name him something like Mikhail, which would be a Russian name."

However, John says that Falcon's art department at the time had misspelled the name on the cover box for the first movie Andrei filmed with them. They had credited Andrei as "Michel Lucas." Since it was already in print on the production art, John and the other decision-makers at Falcon decided to keep Andrei's porn name Michel Lucas throughout his tenure with Falcon. They rationalized it because Michel was a common French name, and Andrei had already done porn in France prior to working with Falcon in America. Andrei eventually changed it from Michel to Michael, but it was at Falcon in 1997 when Andrei Treyvas first acquired a new name.

John felt that Michael was very easy to work with. "I never had a problem with him as a model," John says. "We all got along very well together." For John, the reason he was able to work so well with Michael was a result of their mutual respect. In addition, John saw in Michael the desire to take what he was doing and go as far as he could possibly go. He knew even then that Michael had what it took to become big.

"When it comes to being successful, it really comes down to believing in your product or yourself, and working hard," John says of the gay porn business. "And I think Michael does all of those things." John realized during the taping of Michael's first film with Falcon that Michael had that sort of confidence in himself.

When someone is successful, it can be easy to say in hindsight that he had something that set him apart. However, for John, he truly felt that Michael had a special ambition for what he was doing. In those early days, he could only hope that Michael would continue on that same path. He doesn't claim to have foreseen Michael's current success. But he recalls with clarity that Michael had his own way of doing things, even then. "*Red Alert* was the one where he was on the box cover," John says. "And we did that because of the Russian symbol and the Russian theme."

John felt that when Michael left Falcon, it was because of Falcon's owner at the time, Chuck Holmes. While John really liked working with Michael, thought he did a good job, and thought that he had an interesting look, Holmes did not like Michael's look at all. Holmes didn't like Michael's trademark full lips, nor the way Michael photographed. Holmes didn't even want Michael on the cover box for the Russian-themed film, but John fought for it. "I felt Michael had more potential than Chuck did."

John feels that Michael left Falcon because Holmes didn't like his look and didn't want to continue having Michael as a Falcon exclusive. However, Michael says that, by and large, he did not have a good experience at Falcon.

"They gave me the ugliest guys," Michael recalls. "They would run their sets for eight or nine hours, which was horrible. They would give me this guy with a huge dick, and then a little bottom guy for this three-way, and the big guy would never be able to get hard. So it was hours and hours, and he finally got hard, and then he couldn't cum. It was just a disaster.

"I would never run my sets like that," Michael says now. "If someone cannot work, he's sent home. I remember I never had good-looking partners with Falcon."

Michael didn't complain about his experience with John Rutherford specifically, which says a great deal. If Michael Lucas has an ax to grind, the ax gets ground. Period. He specifically was unhappy with the other models. Also, the way his contract ended after a year was a raw point.

"I think we had a year contract, and that expired," says John. "And we just kind of let it dissolve." Michael ended up not getting paid what he had been promised as a result of Holmes's lack of support for him.

"They were so pissed that I opened my own company that they never bothered to pay me," says Michael, who would start his own company just one year after his first trip to America. "And I was too young and inexperienced, so I didn't want trouble. So I didn't really insist." Michael says that if such a thing were to happen with a company today, "I would destroy them right away.

"I just let it go. They called and said we can give you your movies instead. I brought up the subject two years later, and they gave me VHS copies without boxes, which I threw away eventually, because what can I do with them?"

Michael ended up shooting only five films for Falcon. His titles there included *Maximum Cruise, Basic Plumbing 2*, the Russian-themed *Red Alert* as cover model and star, *High Tide*, and *The Chosen*. In some ways he worked his way up from supporting player to main star (in *Red Alert*), largely because John Rutherford was pulling for him. However, since Holmes wasn't impressed by him, he would never have become a Falcon "star," even though he was signed with them as an exclusive.

"We moved on," John says of both Michael and Falcon. "And Michael and I hadn't really talked about it that much, although we joke about it. But I don't think we actually ever corresponded or communicated about it. It wasn't really conveyed to Michael, either. I don't think I ever told Michael that, and Chuck [Holmes] is not around anymore."

When Michael was still filming movies for Falcon, he never let anyone compromise the things about himself that he felt were important. During filming for *High Tide*, Falcon went on location to Hawaii, where they wanted Michael to do a scene on the beach in the sun. To this day, Michael avoids the sun at all costs, and it was something he wouldn't tolerate even in those early days.

John recalls that, in addition to his refusal to film in the sun, Michael also did his own makeup and hair. He wouldn't allow Falcon's makeup artist to touch him. "Just put some makeup on his face," John would sometimes insist, because Michael couldn't see that he looked very different in the monitor than he had in the mirror when he had applied his makeup. "I remember him being picky about the sun, picky about makeup, and he liked to take control of his own face and how it was presented," John says. "Of course, as a director, I remember that."

"I told them right away," Michael remembers. "I'm not going to sit in the sun and be doing anything in the sun, so they called me a brat all the time. I was not about to fry in the sun and destroy my skin for Falcon Studios. They gave me $1,500. I was not about to do it for $1,500. It was not interesting for me."

Though Michael did not have a good overall experience with Falcon, he recognizes the integral role the experience played in making him who he is today. "I built my name starting with them," Michael states appreciatively. It helped when he eventually started his own company. After he made his first movie on his own, Michael says, "I just started calling all the reviewers and said 'I'm Michael Lucas and I've made my own film.' So they knew who I was already, and that helped. Because you couldn't just call and say you're nobody and that you've made a movie. They wouldn't be excited. So that's how it is."

It would be another year before he would strike out on his own, but he was clearly becoming more confident with his looks, his sexuality, and the direction in which he wanted his career to go. He was also sure, at this point, that moving to America was no longer a future dream, but a present reality that he was ready to deal with.

In Shasha and Shron's *Red Blues*, Yevgeny Ryshik states, "The first year of immigration is a very curious experience. You feel vulnerable, completely insecure, in a new country, surrounded by new people with unfamiliar customs. It's a shock. Then, little by little, you begin to adapt." In *The Soviet Jewish Americans*, Orleck expands on Ryshik's feelings to say that being in a strange new place was the least of the problems faced by most immigrants, "The youngest, strongest, and most adaptable were quickly absorbed into the booming economy of New York in the early 1980s and 1990s. But many of these immigrants experienced rather dramatic downward mobility, at least initially. That downward slide was more common for immigrants in New York than in many other cities."

However, although Michael's first year in America would prove to have its challenges, he would not experience the hardships described by Orleck that other Soviet Jews in New York were facing. This is just one example of Michael's willingness to do anything it takes to get what he wants. It was a trait that Anna saw in him in high school, and that Ivanna had seen in him consistently since the two of them were eight years old.

He had arrived in America as a young gay Russian man who was making his living as an escort in Eastern Europe. But when he boarded the plane after filming his first gay porn film for Falcon, he was returning to Isaiah in New York as Michael Lucas. Even with all his ambition, foresight, and expectations of himself, he did not yet understand all that being Michael Lucas would mean.

13

Every day that Michael was in San Francisco, he and Isaiah talked on the telephone at least twice, for about an hour each time. When Michael did return, the two of them nearly went out of their minds during the six hours that Michael's plane was late getting into New York. The six wasted hours were valuable time, since Michael was set to go back to Munich—and Marco—the next day. But they didn't dwell on the time they had lost. Instead, they made the most of every moment they had together.

"It's crazy," Isaiah said. "But I wish you could come back and stay with me."

"I wish that, too," Michael said. "I want to be with you."

"What about the guy in Germany?"

"I'm not going to stay with him anyway," Andrei said. He had made his mind up about it long before this moment. Maybe Isaiah had something to do with it. Maybe he didn't.

"Then come back here," Isaiah pleaded. "Let's be together. We can see a musical on Broadway every week. This is New York, for fuck's sake!"

Michael laughed, excited by the prospect of living in the cultural center of the world. "You know I love Broadway."

"I love it, too," Isaiah said, saying all the right things. "And we can see every show that gets produced."

"I could make so much money here."

"There's no doubt about it."

Michael and Isaiah's excitement had not diminished at all when Isaiah took Michael to the airport and saw him off the next day. Michael had his mind set on Isaiah, and on America. He'd had a taste and wanted more, wanted it all. There had never been anything Michael Lucas wanted that he couldn't get.

When he arrived in Germany, his youth and his excitement over Isaiah and New York manifested in aggressiveness toward Marco. What seemed like haste was actually the result of four weeks of loving America, four weeks of serious thought about the direction of his life and career, and the two prior years Michael felt he had wasted in Europe.

Within a day, he broke up with Marco and, essentially, ran away from home. He and Marco had been living in their apartment for almost two years by then, and Michael left everything. He packed one bag with a pair of jeans, a few pairs of underwear, and his legal papers. Three days later, he was back in New York, back in the arms of his beloved Isaiah.

Michael didn't know what had happened in the three days he was gone. Perhaps nothing had happened. It was possible that Isaiah hadn't realized how serious Michael had been about actually coming back to live in New York. Maybe Isaiah thought his two-week affair with the hot European porn star was just that—an affair. Because his behavior when Michael returned was a disappointment from day one.

Isaiah was just getting started in business, and as the rookie merchandiser for a major men's clothier, he wasn't making much money. Michael moved in with him in his large studio apartment in the middle of what Michael considered to be the worst part of town, near Times Square. The flat was located on West Fiftieth Street, between Tenth and Eleventh. In Hell's Kitchen in 1997, the neighborhood was full of transsexual hookers. "It was cheap trannies, hustling around," Michael recalls. "And it was a horrible neighborhood. Everything made me just very much depressed. He turned out to be very strange, very moody, and very egotistical."

The day Michael arrived, Isaiah took him to a restaurant for dinner. At the restaurant, an attractive man who worked there approached them and said hello.

"Rod Novoa," Isaiah said, his arm on Michael's back. "This is Andrei Treyvas, my new boyfriend. He's just moved here from Munich."

"It's nice to meet you," Rod said to Michael, seeming to ignore Isaiah's showy behavior. He put his hand out, and he and Michael shook.

"Yes, likewise," Michael said, also overlooking Isaiah's behavior.

"All the way from Munich?" Rod asked. "Is that where you're from originally?"

"No, he's originally from Russia," Isaiah said. "He came here to be with me."

"Congratulations," Rod said genuinely. "Well, I'd better get back to work. It really was nice to meet you."

"You, too," Michael said as Rod left their table.

"He was my first boyfriend," Isaiah said.

"Why did you bring me to the restaurant where he works?" Michael asked, now more uncomfortable than he had been by Isaiah's behavior alone. "I feel a little on the spot."

"No," Isaiah said. "Rod doesn't care. We're still good friends."

As it would turn out, Isaiah and Rod were still *friendly*, which is rather different from still being friends. But Rod was a nice guy, and Michael recognized his sense of style immediately.

The next day was Michael's birthday. Isaiah took him back to the same restaurant. With no surprises this time, they actually had a very good time. Afterward, Michael and Isaiah caught a plane to Georgia, on their way to meet Isaiah's family. "They were very nice people," Michael remembers of his first meeting with the Remingtons. However, he and Isaiah were not allowed to hold hands in front of them, or even touch each other, because they were a very religious Catholic family. "But I had to sit there for four or five hours." Michael would come to understand very quickly that he would have to repeat this visit on a regular basis.

Although his relationship with Isaiah was falling short, Michael continued thinking about his future and planning ahead, and went about getting his existence in order. He got medical insurance and started the process of playing the lottery for a green card. He also went immediately to work, building up clients as an escort in New York City. "That was the biggest money-maker ever," Michael says, debunking the downward mobility trend that other Soviet Jews were experiencing. "I would have about five clients a day. I would make over $1,000 a day, and sometimes it would be much more if I traveled. Sometimes it would be $2,000 and up."

Michael had discovered the Internet and was using it to his advantage as an escort the way he had used the hustler ads in the European magazines. He set up a bank account and began saving every dime he was making as an escort, as well as the money from the few films he was making that first year with Falcon Studios.

Business was good, and Michael had started building a clientele that included celebrities and millionaires. He had very high-end clients whom he respected and admired, along with some who were as sketchy as they come.

Early one morning, a man called, wanting to go to Michael's apartment for a date. This was one of the few times Michael took middle-of-the-night clients before he had learned his lesson about knowing when to shut the phone off. At two o'clock in the morning, good-looking Karim appeared at Michael's door. An hour and a half later, after Michael had performed in top form, Karim got dressed and prepared to leave.

"I'm sorry," said Karim. "I don't have any cash on me tonight."

"Well, you have to pay me," Michael insisted.

"I have checks," Karim said. "I can write you a check for the amount of the date."

Michael had a rule not to take checks, but it was his only option at this point, or not to get paid at all. And Karim was very nice, a genuinely sweet guy. He seemed at least somewhat trustworthy. So Michael took Karim's check.

A few days later, Michael received a notice from his bank that the check Karim had written him had not cleared due to insufficient funds.

"Karim, your check bounced," Michael said calmly on the telephone.

"That's strange," Karim said.

"Well, I have the check. You can bring me the cash, and I'll give the check back to you."

"I can't do that right now," Karim said, losing the sweetness that had made him seem so trustworthy.

"You have to," Michael said, now insisting. "The check bounced, so you have to give me cash now."

"I don't have to give you anything, you illegal immigrant," Karim said, and hung up the telephone.

This situation with Karim was one of three occasions where checks bounced. "There was another situation where the guy didn't pay me," Michael says. "And this guy became a porn star, and I just explained to him that he would not be able to get any work, because I am a distributor, and I would ask all companies I distribute to not to use him. I told him I make these companies hundreds of thousands of dollars; 'what do you think, will they take your side, or will they let you go?'" The porn star brought him all the money.

"One time I took a check from an old man, and he was about ninety years old, and his check bounced," Michael says. "And, you know, I'm not fighting with an old man. I didn't give a fuck. It gave me a lesson. I never, ever would take a check, so that was a lesson."

We often hear horror stories about the tragic circumstances that befall prostitutes of all genders, and of all sexual orientations. In some respects, Michael had it easy. But there were examples such as these where Michael had unpleasant experiences with his escort work. On those rare occasions, Michael did two things. First, he learned his lesson never to make the same mistakes again. And second, he vowed to get what was coming to him.

In his situation with Karim, he vowed never to take checks again. It had always been his policy, but this situation reinforced it in a way that, if a client didn't have the money to pay, Michael would take property in trade. "There were a few young guys who tried to play a trick on me. You walk in and there is a gorgeous boy—*gorgeous*—and he would say, 'I'm sorry. I needed to run to my bank machine, and it didn't give me my money.' If they said it right away, I would walk out." If they waited until it was over and time to pay, Michael would make a different arrangement.

For example, one man gave Michael his expensive watch—rather, Michael took the watch. "I said, 'I'm sorry, I'm taking your watch. And you can pick it up at any time.'"

"Oh, really?" said the man. "Well, I'm gonna call the police now if you don't give me my watch back."

"Okay, go right ahead," said Michael. "You can do it now, or after I leave."

But, of course, he was bluffing about the call to the police. When the man brought Michael the money, Michael returned the watch, and the man apologized. When another man couldn't pay, Michael took all the man's CDs home with him. Later, the man brought Michael the money, and Michael returned the CDs to him. With Karim, Michael put the check in a file and vowed one day to get the money if it was the last thing he would ever do.

So, while Michael was learning how to handle himself as a male escort in America and building a name with the early films he was making for Falcon, his relationship with Isaiah was continuing to fall short of the expectations that had been engendered on Michael's first trip to the United States. It wasn't just Isaiah's erratic behavior or his boring family. Michael could tell that while Isaiah often was very genuinely intimate and compassionate, his heart just didn't seem to be in it.

In April, just two months after Michael and Isaiah had met, Michael arranged for the two of them to take a trip to Russia. Michael had met Isaiah's family, so he wanted Isaiah to meet his family, to whom he was still so very close. Michael had already begun thinking about how to get his family to come to America. As soon as he got his green card, it would finally be possible. In the meantime, a trip to Russia would provide him the chance to see his family, the chance for his new boyfriend to meet them for the first time, and also the chance for Isaiah to see where Michael had grown up. After all, that is one of the best ways to really get to know someone.

PART FOUR

The Marriage of Heaven and Hell

Without Contraries is no progression. Attraction and Repulsion, Reason and Energy, Love and Hate, are necessary to Human existence.
        —William Blake, from *The Marriage of Heaven and Hell*

14

In addition to meeting Michael's family, this was also Isaiah's first trip to Russia, and so was more akin to a vacation than simply a meeting of his boyfriend's family. Michael had earmarked a lot of time for him and Isaiah to see the sights of the country as tourists would do.

Interestingly, Michael and Isaiah took separate flights to Russia, and Isaiah arrived at the airport in Moscow two hours before he was to meet up with Michael. As much as Isaiah was looking forward to his time in Moscow, he would have preferred to be in St. Petersburg instead. However, Michael's parents did not live in St. Petersburg, and meeting them was the main point of his coming to Russia at all.

Isaiah felt his life up to this point had been a happy one, and for him, this trip represented the beginning of the next chapter in his life: a doorway into his thirties, which he looked forward to. He hoped that life as he approached midlife would be as rewarding as the first half had been.

Isaiah had slept for most of the flight to Moscow. While he was awake, he used the time to read. The only other time he woke was at the point when the in-flight meal was being served.

The flight attendant, after giving a welcome speech in

Russian, translated in English what the local time and temperature were in Moscow. Isaiah was shocked to discover that the temperature was approximately 20 degrees, but was comforted by Michael's promise that the weather would become warmer in a few days. As Isaiah stood in the airport of the strange land, surrounded by hundreds of people but no one he knew, a wave of excitement jolted through him. He would see Michael soon, and he would see Russia!

Isaiah was somewhat disturbed by the cold weather, but his excitement about his stay was renewed at the thought of Michael. He was concerned that he might not like Russia, but at least he would see Michael in his homeland. Thoughts raced through Isaiah's head as he stood there at, what he envisioned as, the threshold of the rest of his life.

Michael arrived at the airport on schedule and found Isaiah waiting for him. In Moscow, as in some other countries, the taxi cabs are often private citizens who use the cars they own to make extra money by taking passengers. Such was the cab that Michael hailed at the airport to take him and Isaiah to their destination. The cab took them to the apartment where they were going to stay, which belonged to someone Michael's mother knew.

They took a nap then went to the White House, the site where Communists had been attacked in the early 1990s, and Michael was able to tell Isaiah about the incident from personal experience. They then passed by the Metro station on their way to Michael's mother's house.

Michael's mother made lunch for everyone, and Isaiah met Michael's father, who did not speak English. Isaiah found the exchange more frustrating than interesting. However, he did find Michael's fourteen-year-old brother funny. After lunch and meeting the family, Isaiah watched a Communist propaganda film with them that he also found funny. Then he and Michael went to buy some medicine because Isaiah was getting sick.

In the early evening, they went back to the apartment where they were staying. Isaiah attempted to sleep off his illness for a few hours. When he awoke, he felt somewhat better, but it was snowing outside. Prior to the trip, Michael had told Isaiah that it was stupid for people to think Moscow is always cold.

On their second night in Russia, Michael took Isaiah to the Pushkin Gallery, a place where reproductions of famous statues are located so that Soviets would not have to leave the country to view them. After seeing the artistic representations at Pushkin, Isaiah and Michael paused for a coffee and a shower before going to see *La Traviata* at the Bolshoi. Isaiah didn't care for the performance, but found the theater itself beautiful. Under the influence of the cold medicine, Isaiah fought to stay awake as they then went to gay clubs that he found dull and full of people he hated.

Their third day in Russia was more of the same kinds of things. It was still snowing, and Isaiah's illness had left his sleep fitful and sporadic. Between the snow and being sick, Isaiah was unable to enjoy the lunch that Michael's father had made for them. He ate without complaining, but inwardly Isaiah longed to be able to eat food he could enjoy.

After some time spent looking for plane tickets and taking a nap at the home of a friend of Michael's, the young men went to Manhattan Express, a straight club that Isaiah found boring. Once again, they went by a taxi which was actually a privately owned car. The driver, whom Isaiah described as "thuggish," left him unsettled and made him feel unsafe.

They didn't stay at Manhattan Express long before they proceeded to a different club called Chance, which Isaiah felt was probably the most popular gay club in Moscow. Isaiah hated the music, but danced with Michael's friends and had a good time. Later, they went to a club called the Three Monkeys before going back to the apartment for the night.

The next night, Michael and Isaiah went to see *The*

Nutcracker at the Kremlin Theatre. Isaiah enjoyed the performance, then the two of them went for a walk through the Kremlin. Unfortunately, the weather was still cold in Moscow, and the chill bit through Isaiah. Still, he walked through the historic city with Michael Lucas at his side. They eventually arrived at a restaurant called Angelico's, where they celebrated with the staff of Three Monkeys for their anniversary party. The night had been a full one, and had not been short, but Michael and Isaiah were up early the next morning for a flight to St. Petersburg.

Isaiah's hope that it might be warmer in St. Petersburg was crushed when they arrived to snow. To add insult to injury, Isaiah found out that, since their departure, Moscow had gotten warmer. However, with his Viennese coffee in hand, Isaiah pushed on, determined to enjoy this leg of the trip. He and Michael set off to see some sights, have lunch, visit the Russian Museum, and finish the day with dinner.

The next day, Michael and Isaiah visited the Hermitage Museum. They passed through the exhibits and displays viewing art that Isaiah found pleasing. Michael and Isaiah enjoyed each other's company on the trip, but Isaiah's illness and his aversion to the climate and the food that was strange to him often made him contrary.

Isaiah found the churches fascinating and beautiful, and Michael took him to the theater on their last night in St. Petersburg to see *Don Carlos*. At the theater, a friend of Michael's was able to get them into the performance late and even upgrade their seats after intermission. This exchange at the theater inspired Isaiah to refer to Michael as a "mixed blessing/double-edged sword." On one hand, his boyfriend was the gorgeous, almost-famous porn star Michael Lucas. On the other hand, he realized that Michael was able to get whatever he wanted because of his connections in the sex industry (both on film and on the street).

The two of them spent more time the next day as tourists.

Isaiah found it strange to see locals sunbathing in the cold weather. After three days, Isaiah and Michael prepared to leave St. Petersburg and go back to Moscow.

When Michael and Isaiah got back to Moscow, Isaiah spent the day writing postcards to his family and friends back in the States. On into the day, he and Michael returned to Red Square to see the sights. The two of them had problems because they were not allowed to take their camera into the Lenin Mausoleum, and the area where they were supposed to check the camera was difficult to find.

They ended up leaving their camera with a clerk at a kiosk. They entered Lenin's Tomb. Isaiah found it interesting that they were not allowed to have their hands in their pockets during the tour, and everyone was completely silent. Several guards filled the space, and they eventually passed Lenin's body. Isaiah found that the body looked quite fake, so fake in fact that he imagined it was probably real. It was eerie. Moving on, they then passed a wall where others were entombed, and finally left to visit St. Basil's.

They ate lunch at Michael's grandmother's. Isaiah found the language barrier frustrating. Michael's grandmother only spoke Russian, and Isaiah did not speak or understand Russian at all. They were, however, joined by Michael's brother, Pavel, whom Isaiah enjoyed very much. They also met with another friend of Michael's. Isaiah's comments of the new friend were somewhat condescending, but supportive in that he liked how he dealt with Michael, whom Isaiah described as his "megalomaniacal" mate.

The next day, Isaiah went back to writing more postcards before he and Michael set off again into the city. They met with yet another friend of Michael's and toured an art gallery. They met Pavel again for lunch, then went back to the Bolshoi that evening for a performance of *Giselle*. Isaiah enjoyed the performance, having been surrounded for days by high concentrations of art and culture on the guiding arm of Michael Lucas. Later, they went back to Three Monkeys before going back to the apartment for the night.

On their last day in Moscow, Isaiah bought caviar and plane tickets. He spent a great deal of time that final day with Michael's mother, whom he credited with feeding them so well during the visit. They saw *La Bohème* at the Bolshoi. They had good seats and Isaiah liked the performance. They went again to Angelico's to eat, where Isaiah found the food mediocre but also where he had good memories of his time there with Michael.

Isaiah seemed grateful about the trip and the quality time he had spent with Michael in Russia, but he was bothered that they had spent every second there together. However, he did seem to feel that the trip strengthened their bond. In spite of his illness, the weather, the bad experiences Isaiah had with the food that was so strange to him, the trip would be something that would remain memorable and special to him forever.

Isaiah reflected somewhat critically on Russia as a country, much as anyone would reflect on an obscure place that has been shrouded in mystery and occupied with a nationalistic agenda after seeing it firsthand for the first time.

Isaiah felt that the Cold War went on for too long and that Russia suffered for it. He wondered why it took such a small amount of time for the Communists to destroy their economy and ruin the power of Russia. But even we as Americans can understand how poor leadership does not need much time to turn a surplus into a harsh deficit.

On the Russian people, Isaiah observed that they were very focused on their children. He found that they were strong, but tired, which he felt took happiness out of their frame of reference. After spending almost two weeks in Russia, Isaiah looked forward to the day when the Russian people would have the better life he felt they deserved.

With the trip at its end, Isaiah and Michael flew back to New York on the same flight.

15

"My experience with Isaiah was totally different," says Rod Novoa. Rod is the man who worked in the restaurant that Isaiah took Michael to the first day he arrived in America to stay. "It was like two different people. I didn't even recognize the Isaiah he was after we broke up. It's amazing how people can turn on a dime like that."

During the day, Michael was still escorting and saving all the money he could. "And I was becoming popular," says Michael. "So there were more and more clients who wanted to hook up with me." The new clients had seen Michael in the movies he was doing for Falcon and were willing to pay much more than Michael had been getting up until that point. At night, Michael spent all his time with Isaiah. Isaiah wanted Michael to stop seeing all the friends he had outside the relationship. Michael, who was obsessively in love with Isaiah, agreed.

Although most of Michael's escort clients were serviced during the day, there were a few that would pay as much as $3,000 for an overnight date. For them, Michael made exceptions. The first thing Michael used his money for was to pay all his legal expenses to become legal in the country—and for clothing. "Of course, I was buying clothes, always," Michael recalls. "I was always buying good pieces, which I still have." The rest of his money went into savings until he had managed to put aside $100,000.

After having been in America for only a year, Michael took his savings and invested it in a company of his own. And in 1998, Lucas Entertainment was born. In *In Harm's Way: The Pornography Civil Rights Hearings*, Andrea Dworkin and Catharine MacKinnon put together a series of court transcripts and documents in an attempt to prove the evils of pornography. However, a lot of the testimony presented makes a good argument in favor of good porn.

In "The Minneapolis Hearings," where Linda Lovelace testified that she was coerced into performing in *Deep Throat* and essentially raped, Tim Campbell testified on behalf of the gay community on December 12, 1983, saying, "Basically we agree on goals. I would like to see queer bashing stopped. I would like to see sexual assault on women stopped. I fear, however, this ordinance [to ban pornography] will only increase the amount of weirdo pornography coming out from the makers. In the last twelve years there has been a change in the production of gay pornography. In early 1970 it was difficult to find anything but really sleazy, shoddy-looking models and a whole lot of abusive stuff in gay pornography. With the movement towards liberation and greater access and larger market, normal adult males consenting in adult sex, there is more of it than there was in 1970."

Campbell's argument, that outlawing porn would only serve to make the industry more dangerous, allows for the possibility that porn that is produced under responsible conditions can have a significant value in society. When Michael started Lucas Entertainment, he raised the bar of porn production to a new high, requiring all his models to undergo drug testing prior to shooting. Campbell's argument, combined with Michael's policies, creates a new image of porn production that negates its seedy stereotype.

It would be another year before Michael would stop escorting. By the year 2000, Michael kept only a few of his good clients, but all his escorting ads came down in 1999. After four years of escorting full time, and using the money to invest in his own fledgling adult film company, Michael had gained a lot of experience on the streets.

"The German experience was a little crazy because Marco, who was a bartender in a restaurant, had a car and would drive me to bars," Michael recalls. "So my own boyfriend was driving me to clients, which is kind of sick." In addition to assisting with Michael's escorting career in terms of driving him, Marco's German was perfect, so he was also making appointments for Michael.

The arrangement didn't bother Michael at all, nor did it bother Marco. The two of them were making a lot of money with the arrangement, and they liked the money and the apartment it afforded them. The apartment was huge and had a garden, and Marco was free to use all the money he wanted, and he did, so Marco was living well off Michael's prostitution.

When Michael left Marco and came to America to be with Isaiah, Michael even continued sending money back to Marco in Germany so that Marco could continue living in the apartment. Marco wouldn't have been able to afford it any other way.

"In America, it was different," Michael says of escorting. "People were richer than in Europe. It was during the Clinton administration, when money was nothing; everybody had it." When Lucas Entertainment first hung out its shingle, Michael had calls every day from people who were seeking to invest in the company. However, Michael wasn't interested in selling off any bits of his dream. This is why he continued escorting for a year after starting the company, so that he could support it completely on his own.

This changed the dynamic of his relationship with Isaiah in some ways. During the day, Michael worked at building his business. In the evenings and on weekends, he was hustling. All the money he made was continuously put back into Lucas Entertainment.

Building a porn business from the ground up is not as easy as it sounds. It's not like Michael bought a camcorder at Circuit City and had a couple of friends doing amateur sex shots in a motel room. There are professional considerations to be made on a daily basis in an industry where not all the players are in it to make a good name for themselves. Many of them are there to make their quick cash and move on. This made it even harder for Michael, who planned to be in it for the long haul.

Every day, Michael was scouting locations (which is still problematic today, even though he is so well established), searching for models every way he could with everything from advertisements to checking out strip clubs. On a daily basis, Michael was poring over lighting, distribution, equipment, permits, art direction, and a million other details.

With four or five a day, most of the names and faces of Michael's escorting clients faded into the daily fog just like any other job would in which volume is the way to generate cash. Michael became the Henry Ford of the sex assembly line, a revolving door of cock and cash, all which went into business and savings. "As I walk down the street," Michael says now, "I'm sure there are people who recognize me because they were clients, because there must have been hundreds of them. But I don't remember them."

However, there were some circumstances that just have a way of burning themselves into a person's memory. "When you escort every day, you get so used to it that you basically get your hard-on automatically, like your dick rising up from a touch—in my case," Michael says. Michael, who never bottomed for his clients, took for granted the fact that he was able to get an erection at any time, in any circumstance. Michael says that he was grateful there was no need—no demand—for him to get fucked by a client. "A lot of escorts have these terribly destroyed assholes," Michael says. "Which is a problem a lot of women have when their whole pussy is falling to their knees. Well, in my case, I was strictly a top with my clients. I always used condoms, so I never got any disease, ever—not even bugs, which is surprising, even to me."

Michael feels that since his clients were able to pay the high rate he charged for a date, they were clean people. These are a very different sort, Michael rationalizes, from the nasty, underbelly people who go to sex clubs. "But it could also be because I never did any drugs," Michael admits. "I was always in control, because it's kind of a dangerous job."

"One guy I'll never forget," Michael recalls of his days on the street, "is this guy who was staying in the Pierre Hotel. It was a beautiful hotel. He was a married man in his sixties. He had no legs, and he was in a wheelchair, so I had to help him get on the bed. He told me that he had been in a car accident, and was stuck between two cars, and it cut his legs off. He had one foot attached to the piece of his leg. And I asked him, 'Why did you do that?' He said, 'The doctor told me the foot was in good condition, so we can try to grow it together. I wouldn't mind having my foot, rather than throwing it away.' And he thought it was a good idea.

"That's not why I remember him, because I saw hundreds of people with different sorts of problems. Some people were enormously fat, but I don't remember them specifically. Him I remember for one reason—for what he said."

"Tell me," the man said. "Are you gay?"

"Yes, I am gay."

"Oh, that's very good."

"Why is that good, sir?" Michael asked the man.

"Because I want the escort to have fun as well," he answered.

"And I looked at him straight," Michael says. "And thought, how far away this man is from reality. Here is a man in his sixties, old, fat, with no legs, with his foot attached basically to his torso. And he thinks that just because I'm gay, I will have fun just because he is male. At this point he can have sex with a woman—with a fat woman. You can have sex with a doorknob. You can have sex with a goat. It doesn't matter, because it's nothing about sexy. It's nothing about hot.

"You're getting a hard-on just because [it's your job]. I don't know how to explain why I could always get a hard-on. But I was young. I had a good sexual energy, and maybe because it was just part of my job where I could get hard. It was an instinct when I was with a client. And I was not disgusted by the appearance of the clients. I didn't focus on that. Also, I'm not one who was thinking about some hot sex that I had with some hot guy. I was just doing this, sticking it in, pulling it out, letting them suck my dick. It was just always hard, maybe because I was never on drugs or drunk, just a healthy guy. But I remember this guy very well because I was stunned. In what kind of unreal world does he live—thinking that I will actually have fun because I'm gay and he's male? He wouldn't have been attractive to anyone. He maybe could be a fetish beast for someone. I've heard of fetishes of this kind, but I don't have this fetish."

When clients called Michael, they would often give him tons of reasons why they might be having to pay for sex. Some would tell him that they didn't have a leg. They would ask if it would be a problem because they were in their eighties or nineties. They would even say things like, "I have AIDS," or "I'm black," or "I'm Asian . . . Is that a problem?" But for Michael, as long as their money was green, it didn't matter. Always safe, always in control, and always hard, Michael took their money and gave them the time of their lives.

On the other hand, however, there was another group of clients who expected free sex from him just because they were young and good-looking. Michael remembers, "I said, 'That's great. I charge 200 an hour.' Or at the point where I became a porn star, I was saying, 'I'm charging 300 an hour.' And at some point, I said, 'I'm charging 350 or 400 an hour.'" But it didn't work when they tried to use their sexy bodies as payment in itself. "Because I always remembered I was working," Michael says. "It's not about fun. It is good when it is fun, but this is about making money. So this second category of people who were going on about how cute they were and trying to break the price, that didn't work with me either. I never did break the price for anyone."

"There was another group of people who, their first question was, 'Do you party?'" Michael says. "And if you tell them no, they hang up on you. So there are a lot of escorts who agree to party [use drugs with clients], and when they go there, they party. And then they have sex, and [possibly] fuck raw. It's just asking for trouble in many ways—to not get paid, to be abused.

"I never had those bad experiences, and I never put myself in those situations. I'm sure there are many escorts who can tell you wonderful stories about that. I did see drug addicts, but it would be very rare. Because when they ask me on the phone if I party and I say no, they still wanted to see me because I'm Michael Lucas. But when you get there, they either have a lot of money and you will be able to get all of it—because they're stoned, paranoid, time flies, and they just keep giving you money—or they will be completely broke. All they will have is crystal [the drug crystal meth], and they will offer you their furniture, their clothes, their chandelier, which you don't want.

"Then there were people, I got very good with the phone, and there were all these calls from people who were completely stoned. And the kind of client who was stoned—especially on crystal—for a while, I did them. The advantage of it is that you could get anything from them, whatever they have, all their money. I would end up leaving with $2,000 or $3,000. But a lot of times, you get there and realize they don't have a dime. So, after a while, I just stopped dealing with these types of clients, and I never went to clients who called on drugs."

In *The Soviet Jewish Americans*, Orleck states, "Most of those who came in the 1970's have by now grown accustomed to life in the United States. Whether they speak flawless, barely accented English or continue to communicate primarily in Russian, it has been at least twenty years since most of them held Soviet citizenship. They have come to feel settled in their American lives." However, it did not take Michael nearly that long to realize that this is where he belonged, and that he would be successful here without a doubt.

16

Just five months after the trip he took with Michael to Russia, Isaiah embarked on a pair of trips to Europe while Michael stayed in the United States.

During the last part of September, Isaiah flew to London for the first of the two trips. Upon his arrival, he ordered what he assumed to be a traditional English breakfast, only to receive underdone eggs and dry toast. He enjoyed the coffee he was served, but was disappointed that the breakfast he had hated cost more than twenty dollars.

Isaiah flew to London to celebrate the birthday of a friend, and he had a wonderful time. Unfortunately, however, what Isaiah seemed to remember most about the trip was not the fellowship and camaraderie of his friends. Instead, he mostly focused on specific times and cab rides. He reflected mostly on the food he ate, the music he listened to, the hotel where he stayed, and the naps he took. The devil *is* in the details.

On his own, he visited the British Museum and the Rosetta Stone. He gushed that his friends lived in the same neighborhood as Sting and Annie Lennox, and in the afternoon on his first day in England, he beat his friend Daniel at tennis.

He visited Marx's grave, a figure whom Isaiah admired. For Isaiah, this was the shortest trip to London he had ever taken. He enjoyed the city and brought home good memories of being there, but at the same time was detached from the positive aspects of the culture and seemed to have little emotional attachment to his friends. Although he had been to London before, Isaiah still visited all the tourist traps unlike someone familiar to the city would do.

Only a month later, his second of the two trips found Isaiah in glorious and romantic Paris, France—again, sans Michael.

Isaiah went to Paris to visit his friend, Paul, who managed a famous comedian. He was proud of himself that he had gone to Europe so much recently.

Paul had a home in Paris, and upon his arrival, Isaiah waited at the home of one of Paul's friends while she went to pick him up. Isaiah ate cheese, drank coffee, and took a nap. As it was with London, Isaiah had previously spent time in Paris as well. In fact, it was with his friend Geoff that he had spent time in Paris before. This was Isaiah's first trip to Paris without Geoff.

Isaiah enjoyed that he was able to shop while he was there, and was impressed by the food he had at a restaurant he described as "very French." On his second day there, he and his friend did more shopping and visited the Picasso Museum. They ate lunch, took a nap, and went to dinner at a fancy seafood restaurant, where he was impressed by the captain tasting the wine for them. He enjoyed the dinner and the conversation.

Also similar to his London trip, the Paris trip was short. After only two days, Isaiah had to leave the City of Love. He missed having Geoff there, but it was as if having Michael there never even crossed his mind. Isaiah felt that the trip was a smooth one, but wished he could have done more. However, his friend Paul, or "Paulie" as he affectionately called him, was over seventy and couldn't do as much as someone in his twenties. Isaiah left Paris hoping to see more sights the next time.

Growing up the way he did—while not an excuse—does serve as an explanation for Isaiah's state of mind. When Michael was exposed to Isaiah's family, it often resulted in drama that Michael rejected loudly. In the way that Isaiah's upbringing (as you will soon see) can explain his current state of mind, Michael's Russian Jewish upbringing was conducive to the way he finds it impossible to keep his mouth shut—which, of course, is why we love him.

17

As it turned out, Isaiah's escapades to Europe weren't just friendly visits. Michael discovered that Isaiah was hustling as well. This wouldn't necessarily be a bad thing, because Michael was a hustler. The difference was that they both knew Michael was a hustler and a porn star. Michael never tried to hide it.

Eventually, it came to Michael's attention that Isaiah had been hustling since long before he had arrived. Isaiah's nervousness at the photo shoot when he first met Michael now seemed less than genuine—and more like a lie, a manipulation.

"He was also a hustler through one of the agencies in New York City," Michael recalls. "Where they were giving him a lot of really good clients. One of his clients was this guy who was the manager of a famous stand-up comic—this married guy.

"He had a lot of famous clients, and I became friends with them, it's crazy, in the future when we broke up. He was always very much interested in other people. It's funny that all these people were Jews and Isaiah was very anti-Semitic. His family was very anti-Semitic, and I understood then that if you have a boyfriend who is Jewish, it doesn't automatically mean that you are not anti-Semitic. You can have a Jewish boyfriend and be anti-Semitic. You don't have to be very prejudiced to be attracted to Michael Lucas. I just happened to be sexy."

But the anti-Semitism that Isaiah harbored (and covered well in most circumstances) became a growing problem between him and Michael. "He was intelligent enough to cover it all to a certain point," Michael says. "The way he would talk, it wouldn't be that Jews are bastards. That came later, when he would be angry at me. But that was much later.

"But the first year it would be lines like, 'I really don't like New York Jews. All they can think about is their money.' And at the same time, he would have Jewish friends. But he would always say things like, 'It's always easy to figure out the bill with my Jewish friends,' and stuff like that. I could never understand what kind of person he really was. Was he good? Was he bad? There were too many colors in him."

These conflicts led to a breakup in 1998, just as Michael was starting Lucas Entertainment. He and Isaiah had a huge fight over one of the girls Michael had met when he had first come to America, at the restaurant where he met Isaiah's ex, Rod. Thinking back to that meeting, Michael had thought it awkward that he and Isaiah had to sit there with these girls and act like two straight guys when he had just left his boyfriend in Germany to be in America with Isaiah.

What Michael found out later was that one of the girls was Isaiah's ex-girlfriend, and that the two of them used to get together, do coke, and fuck. So, when Isaiah told Michael on his first day here that they needed to act like they were just friends, he had said, "They're from my work, you know. These people don't need to know."

It didn't take Michael long to realize that Isaiah was an alcoholic. "He couldn't go on unless he had three to four

Stoli martinis in the evening," Michael says. "And this is very typical of guys who grow up in a very Catholic family. That's what they are; that's how they are. When you're being suppressed by your family all the time, it all comes out in an ugly way. Everything was just depressing. I could count the days when I was really happy.

"It was all a big disappointment, and I was really depressed in this studio apartment with no friends. I didn't know anyone, my English was bad, and Isaiah was always being mean, being rude.

"He had all these dinner dates and overnight dates with all these rich clients of his. So the big fight was when he called me and said he was going to dinner with his girlfriend, whom he said was just a friend, and back then I didn't have keys to his apartment."

"Let's meet around ten-thirty or eleven at home," Isaiah said to Michael.

So Michael went to visit a Russian friend of his who was now in New York, and his boyfriend. When they got ready to go to bed, Michael called Isaiah.

"We're about ready to leave the restaurant," Isaiah said. "We just finished dinner and we went to the bar, and we don't feel like rushing. How about I call you when we're about to leave?"

"Okay," Michael agreed and hung up the phone. Then he realized it was raining outside, he had nowhere to go, and his friends were going to sleep. He called Isaiah back and got his voice mail. "Listen, Isaiah. This is absolutely ridiculous. I'm not going to be able to tolerate that. I moved to this country for you, and you are letting me sit in the street because you don't feel like leaving the bar and your good time. I'm sorry I don't have keys to your apartment, but you can't leave me outside."

Michael stood waiting outside the apartment in the rain for forty minutes. At that point, Isaiah arrived and walked slowly up to him and said, "I was going to leave earlier, but I got such a jerk-off message from you, I decided not to rush."

Michael didn't say a word as the two of them walked up to the apartment. Once inside, Michael started packing his bags.

"Please stay," Isaiah said.

"Okay, fine," Michael agreed. "But you really can't be this way."

After twenty minutes more had passed, Isaiah said, "You really didn't mean to leave. Because when someone means to leave, he leaves."

"He was fucking with my brain," Michael says now of that first big fight. "So one day I just had to leave and I left. It was such terrible abuse. I did miss him very much, and that was really crazy. It was the middle of the night. We had a big fight, and I had to leave and didn't have a place to go. That was really the toughest time in New York. So I stayed in a hotel.

"I had to escort like crazy to pay for the hotel and save money. So Marco came from Germany and brought some money, and I made some money. He moved from Germany to New York because he missed me and he was in love with me. I did already like New York, but I could get an apartment only by paying cash. I had no papers, and neither did Marco. We were both, essentially, tourists. I could get the apartment when I paid $16,000 cash, which included six months rent, two months deposit, and fees for the agency. It was the only way I could get the place in the West Village. I was working—I had five to seven clients a day and eventually made the $16,000, and Marco and I got the apartment."

However, Marco had to go on a trip to Germany. He planned to be gone for five days, but it turned out that he would be gone much longer. Isaiah came over to the apartment while Marco was gone and spent the night with Michael. He turned on the charm and made himself into the man Michael had really wanted. "My God!" Michael said. "I was dreaming about this moment, and it just happened. Things will change." Michael reunited with Isaiah, and told Marco to stay in Germany, but kept the apartment he had worked so hard to afford.

After the breakup and, subsequently, the makeup, Michael and Isaiah went to Puerto Rico together. "The first day we were there, he was a complete asshole to me. He became very cold and moody. He wouldn't talk to me, and was very rude to me. At some point, I got frustrated and pushed him away from me. I didn't hit him, just pushed him, and he turned it into a complete nightmare for me. I didn't know he was bluffing—he was bluffing all the time—but I took him seriously when he said, 'I can't be with you anymore. You are violent.'

"So I was really, really down and truly sorry. I apologized for days and days saying, 'Please, I really didn't mean anything. I'm not violent. I will never touch you again.' But he wouldn't give up. He was so cruel. I don't know if he was naturally cruel—I don't think so—but something was going on with him that I didn't know about, and wouldn't have understood even if I had known. What I didn't realize with the pushing incident is that his reaction was all a bluff—a manipulation.

"Things did change," Michael recalls. "Because he was afraid I would leave again and he was trying to get me back."

18

It was a good thing that Michael's escorting experiences were going relatively well. It was never anything that he couldn't handle. Not all of Michael's escort clients were on drugs, missing limbs, or trying to scam him into a lower price. In fact, those clients were the exception to the rule. Michael recalls, "There were a lot of great people—businessmen out of town, or New York businessmen, who would never argue about price, which I was always considering incredibly cheap." Michael says that even though there were clients who tried to bring the price down, his good clients (businessmen with money) never questioned it. "And these were the best people.

"There are escorts who try to find out first where the person is staying, and trying to get more money because they can stay in an expensive hotel. To me, it didn't matter. I never asked first. I told them my price right away."

Michael encountered another group of people who would ask him on the phone, "Do you fuck?"

"Yes," Michael would answer.

"How do you like to fuck?" they would then ask.

Michael says, "The question 'How do you like to fuck?' means either they want to have phone sex right now and talk about sex, or they mean, are you fucking raw, or with a condom? If they ask if you like to fuck raw, if you tell them you only fuck with condoms, as soon as you tell them that, eighty percent of them will hang up.

"I will never forget this one guy. He called me at eleven o'clock and I told him it would cost $400. And he started negotiating, he said, '$350.' I said, '$350 is fine,' and made a mental note to cut the time short. So I went there, and it was the best part of town—Upper West Side. It was an amazing building, and this guy had eight rooms, and was a millionaire. And he even had a small pool in the apartment. He opened the door, dressed incredibly chic, with a glass of wine in his hand.

"He was an Italian man of about forty-five years old— *beautiful.* I didn't ask him why he was negotiating with me. And then he saw me several more times, and he would give me $100 extra, and he saw me about ten times. He finally said he wanted to be my boyfriend, and felt that he should stop paying. I never forgot how cheap he was on that first call."

Michael's first production for Lucas Entertainment, *Back in the Saddle*, was filmed on this client's land. So the man started to feel a sense that Michael owed him something in return, in the form of a bona fide relationship.

"We're going out. I'm taking you to nice dinners and shows," said the man. "You're my boyfriend, and I don't think I should pay your escort fee anymore."

"It's not possible," Michael said.

"Why not?"

"I would never be able to be with someone who is that cheap."

"What do you mean cheap?" he asked. "I take you to the best restaurants, drive you around in the best car. We get the best seats in the opera. What do you mean cheap?"

"On our first meeting, you were negotiating over $50. You have five cars. You're a millionaire, and you're negotiating $50. How can I be a boyfriend of someone like that?"

"Well, I think we're dating now."

"No," Michael said firmly. "We're not dating. You have to pay me. You don't have to pay $900 or $1,000. You can pay the regular rate of $400." So he and Michael never saw each other again.

"I remember one situation," says Michael. "When I actually did hit a guy. I was really tired. He had come to my place around one in the morning, and he came [got off] in ten minutes."

"I need my money back," said the man. "At least seventy percent of it."

"Why?" Michael asked.

"Because I already came, and you charge for the hour."

"You are welcome to hang around me and you can suck my dick, or I can fuck you. I don't care," Michael said. "Or we can have a glass of water together. I don't care; this is not my problem. You made this appointment, and this appointment has to give me $300. Otherwise, if not for you, someone else would be scheduled. And you should understand those things."

"I'm not gonna leave without my money," said the man, and he began walking toward Michael.

Michael was tired, it was the middle of the night (when Michael rarely saw clients anyway), and Isaiah was gone, so Michael was at home alone. As the man approached farther and faster, Michael balled up a tight fist and thrust it forward. When his fist made contact with the client's face, the man was forced backward, and his head upturned at an awkward angle as he stumbled.

When the man regained his bearings and composure, he

left Michael's apartment. "He even forgot his jacket," Michael recalls. "Which he never came to pick up. That was one unpleasant moment." But it wouldn't be his last.

"There was another guy who didn't tell me anything on the phone," says Michael. "But when I got to his place, it was a horrible apartment, with two dogs. The guy was without one leg, and was paralyzed, and you could see his AIDS clearly. What he wanted, really, was to kiss me. But he had herpes on his lips and I said, 'I'm sorry. I don't kiss.' And I don't usually kiss clients. You can't kiss five people a day."

When it was over, the man said, "I'm really not happy. I'm pissed. I've had a horrible life. I lost my leg when I was seven, then I got AIDS, and I sit here with my two dogs taking all these drugs."

"You know what," Michael said. "You don't have to pay." Michael felt such pity for the man. And all he wanted to do at that point was to get out of there, away from the client's terrible sadness, away from his sad stories, and away from his shitty apartment. "I didn't take the money," Michael says now. "Not even for him, but for myself, because I didn't feel good about it. So, I got away from that place, and he called me back in three days. I recognized his voice. He didn't tell me who he was."

"Hi, I'm calling about your service," he said. "I would like to see you tonight."

"What is your address?" Michael asked, already knowing it.

The man gave Michael the address.

"Wait a minute," Michael said. "I did see you three days ago."

"Yes."

"But wait a second. You were not satisfied with my service. You were not happy because I don't kiss, and I didn't take your money because of that. Why are you calling me back if you didn't like me?" The man hung up, so Michael called him back right away. "Why did you hang up on me? I didn't do anything bad to you. I actually spent an hour with you and didn't take your money. So why did you hang up on me right now if I didn't do anything bad? I told you I'm not kissing, and since it was apparently something you care about, I didn't charge you. I'm not able to give you time, and come again for free, because I still wouldn't kiss. If I come, you can pay, but you told me kissing was everything for you. That's what you said. And so why would you pay me if kissing is everything?"

"I'm sorry about that," the man said, defeated. "I'm just in a bad mood, and I apologize."

After they hung up, Michael wondered to himself why he had called him back. "What point did I have to prove?" Michael says now. "That would happen to me sometimes in my life, where I do something and ask myself later why I did it."

19

Tumultuous would be an understatement. Here you have a relatively young man, twenty-six years old, who grew up with a scorned nationality and a scorned sexual orientation in one of the most oppressive environments in history. After experimentation with relationships with men and women, he makes his money on the streets, for sex with men who have problems most of us could barely look at. Now, alone in a new country, he returns to an abusive relationship with a man who lies to him more often than not. Yet he opens his own business in a multibillion-dollar industry that can be devastatingly competitive, unforgiving, and demoralizing.

The only possible way to make this successful is to make your own rules—they must be strict, and you must stick to them at all costs. And you must possess an indeterminate, intangible something within yourself that will never let you stop going after what you want.

"If you have looks, if you have a big dick, if you go to the gym, you will make it," says Michael of men who want to break into gay porn. "It's a very competitive industry. The first thing I found out was that New York was not explored really well. There were a few companies that were producing crappy movies—no quality, and very ethnic, either *just* black or *just* Latin. So, I decided there's a good niche here for, first, quality and, second, multinational and multiracial productions with white guys, Latin guys, black guys—guys from all over the world." Michael was after men who were cut (circumcised) or uncut, different body types, different shapes. "Good shapes," he says. "But different shapes.

"All my guys have to have good bodies," Michael says. But the age differences and the body structure differences were necessary for the look Michael wanted to create. "It's not about body builders; it's not about twinks. It's about everybody. Just like New York. We party together here, and my movies reflect that.

"The first movie I did on my own was *Back in the Saddle*. It took lots of time. It took two or three weeks to make. I had only one cameraman and the best still photographer. The cameraman was kind of irresponsible, and he did only three movies for me; then I switched him for another person. But it was a very challenging experience because I didn't know much, and there were a lot of problems occurring all the time.

"I had a very wealthy client back then who had a huge piece of property somewhere upstate New York or Pennsylvania. We drove there, and he had horses and beautiful forests. So we did this movie, which turned out to be beautiful. It had several scenes and was very nice. I got lots of award nominations for that movie, so it was very successful."

However, starting out can be difficult and can present daily challenges that, in the big picture, often fly under the radar. "It's very difficult," Michael says. "When you just start a company, nobody wants to help you. Back in '98, I would call companies and tell them I wanted to duplicate 500 VHS copies, and nobody would know who I was. Nobody would be interested in giving me their good price or in treating me well."

But apart from the day-to-day challenges of running a business, Michael had the arduous task of developing a brand. He had cornered the New York niche, as most other companies were producing gay porn on the West Coast. But Michael had to figure out how to push elements that were taboo, even in an industry that seemed to be as exposed and uninhibited as gay porn. Michael took his in-your-face background into his film production in such a way that he not only got away with taboos; people loved it.

"There are productions that are only producing the kink stuff," Michael says of integrating hardcore elements into gay porn. "To be honest, those guys can be very ugly. The guys in my movies are very beautiful. My guys, when they're doing that (things like watersports or fisting), it's sexy. It's erotic.

"There's nothing wrong; it's just piss. It's just something that comes out of a dick, and many people love it. It can be very erotic. It's just part of you, and it's what our customers want to see. We give it to them with pleasure because a lot of my guys like to do it. And if they don't, I never force them to do that. There's a questionnaire that asks them what they like to do, and what they don't like to do. They answer it, and I match them, and make them do things based on their paperwork."

It all sounds very official. Artist agrees to get pissed on. Model will piss on other models, but will not take a man's fist and arm up his ass. So perhaps it's not the same kind of rider artists use for an appearance on *20/20*. But it keeps Michael Lucas's sets running smoothly. And it's this kind of atmosphere that makes Michael's sets the antithesis of exposés on seedy porn production.

"I never had bad experiences working in porn because I

was working only for top companies, and only for a very short time," Michael explains. "I can imagine that if there were—and there probably are—companies where people might have had bad experiences with directors or producers, or I don't even know. I can tell you one thing: on my set there is a strict no-drug policy.

"In fact, we test our models for drugs. The model simply has to submit to a urine test for five party drugs. There is a test that provides information on marijuana, ecstacy (X), crystal, and a couple of others. I've never even touched drugs in my entire life, neither cigarettes nor drugs. I can have a glass of red wine occasionally, but never tried any kind of drugs. But if any of these five drugs show positive, the model is fired and will never return to our set again. He would not be paid.

"Well, actually he would not even be able to start, because this is a number-one thing. If he has two scenes, he will be tested twice. So it's very simple. If the model refuses to do it, he's not going to be able to work. There is an agreement he has to sign two weeks before we shoot the movie, that he knows that he's going to be tested, and knows that whatever he does five days prior to shooting will show positive on the test.

"I don't care what they do in their private lives, if they party, if they don't party. I mean, I would wish very much that nobody did drugs; that's my campaign. But I can't control their lives. So all I care about is that they look good, fresh, get enough sleep, and one week before they start, they cannot touch drugs.

"I have a perfect adult world where everything is, with the help of my office, everything is already set up and lined up so that it is very clean, and we're not running into any trouble. Because whenever someone is on drugs, that's where there's trouble."

In addition to his policy on drugs, Michael demands a

standard from his models that requires a genuine portrayal of gay sex. Many directors hire models who say they are straight, creating an entire subgroup of gay porn models who insist that they only have gay sex on film for the money. These "gay-for-pay" models are so vocal about their supposed straight sexuality, that it is often assumed that *most* gay porn models are actually straight. However, this is not the case. And directors who set the bar higher, like Michael Lucas, do not use models who can't genuinely perform sexually with men.

"I don't know them; I don't use them," Michael says of gay-for-pay models. "For me, it's all about being real. You can't fake good sex. If someone is coming to me, and he is straight, it's not interesting. I don't care what you call yourself. You can call yourself gay, straight, or bi. When I was filming in Moscow, the Russian men all said they were straight. Well, they lied. They were all gay. I don't care what you think about yourself, but they all enjoyed fucking each other up the ass. That's what I want."

As much as Michael tried to put into building his business, Isaiah was sabotaging his efforts at every turn. The attention Isaiah needed and the demands he was placing on Michael interfered a great deal with what Michael was trying to accomplish. Although Michael was making progress financially with the business because he was still escorting, he was beginning to understand that it would not flourish to its full potential as long as he was with Isaiah.

20

Gay Pride Day is a time of emotions running wild for gay citizens all over the world. It is a time when we are proud of how far we've come, and when we get recharged for the political and social work that is yet to be done. It is a time for many families to bond, and for others—just striking out on their own—to develop new families: dear friends of their choosing who include a network of brothers, sisters, and adoptive mothers and fathers. Centuries of our existence in the face of oppression—masked with religion, politics, and hate—culminate into one day that says we are, in fact, here—and queer.

It was on Gay Pride Day, his emotions as full as any other New Yorker waving a flag or donning a wig, when Michael discovered that his beloved Isaiah had a substance abuse problem. Isaiah was supposed to meet Michael at the apartment he had kept.

"I fell asleep," Isaiah said. "I'm sorry. I'll be there in half an hour."

An hour later, when Isaiah still hadn't arrived, Michael phoned him again. "Where are you?"

"I'm on my way," Isaiah assured him. "Just another half hour."

Again, Isaiah did not arrive. "I think it took me three hours of this crazy phone tag, and I suddenly realized something is going wrong," Michael remembers. "I think he wanted me to see and understand that he was on drugs because he kept saying, 'Just don't come here. I'll come there.'

"So, of course, I went there, and he wouldn't open the door. That's when I suspected he was doing drugs. I started to knock on the door so hard that all the neighbors heard. So he had to open the door, and I saw him in a horrible state with his eyes completely out. I had never seen anything like it."

A week later, Michael moved Isaiah into his apartment. Feeling as if he could help Isaiah win the fight against drugs, Michael became Isaiah's enabler, and would continue in that role for the next two years.

Every two to three weeks, Isaiah would disappear all night, not returning to Michael's apartment until five or six o'clock in the morning. When he finally did get home, he would be shaking and crying. There were even a few times when his state would be so horrifying, Michael took him to the hospital.

At the same time, Isaiah was working every day. He left at seven every morning to attend meetings, visit department stores, assist with advertising, and even help prepare in-store merchandise displays. In the evenings, he and Michael would attend either the opera or the theater, or they would visit an exhibition at a museum. "It was a good, cultural life with him," Michael says. "And he was incredibly smart. At the same time, however, I was fighting with him over his drug addiction.

"The longest he could go without drugs was a month. Then, he would disappear again for the whole night and come home in this absolutely horrible condition." Michael forced Isaiah to attend several different meetings, and would be with him the entire time. However, the meetings didn't change anything, and eventually Isaiah started going to a psychiatrist.

A former client of Isaiah's, a Catholic priest named James who had a significant position in a Catholic church upstate, tried to help as well. Eventually, Isaiah stopped escorting, but kept a few of his former clients as friends, as was the case with Father James.

As Isaiah had stopped escorting, he became very jealous and controlling over Michael's career with Lucas Entertainment, forbidding him to appear in his own films. "His thing was to keep me away from my success, all for himself," Michael says. "That was very much him. I understood at some point that's another thing I never will get myself into again: someone who will keep me away from my success, who would be jealous of my success for one or another reason. It's difficult to have control over someone who is famous. So he was always making sure I had people to do the movies."

One particular morning at six o'clock, Isaiah had still not returned home after an all-night binge. Michael was extremely worried about him, more so than on usual nights. "So I called his oldest sister. His sister and her boyfriend then became aware of the situation and told his father about it."

The relationship between Michael and Isaiah's family had never been a good one. After Michael involved them in Isaiah's addiction, the situation did not improve, not even enough for them to thank Michael for trying to take care of him. During the holidays, Michael was walking through Central Park with Isaiah's father when they came upon a large menorah that had been placed in the park for the holiday.

"My God, Mr. Remington," Michael said to Isaiah's father. "That would never be possible in Moscow, to have a menorah in the center of Moscow of this size. America is such a great country, such a tolerant country."

"Well," Mr. Remington said, "in the very same country, there are people who threw a Virgin Mary statue out of a church."

Realizing where he was going with the story, and certain that Mr. Remington had either made it up completely, or at the very least did not have details of the incident, Michael said, "Who did? Who did it?"

"Well," Mr. Remington answered. "Liberals and Jews."

"Why would you say that to me?" Michael asked. "It hurts that you would say that."

Situations like these were becoming increasingly frequent with Isaiah's family. For example, at Christmas dinner while Michael and Isaiah were in Georgia visiting, Isaiah's youngest sister said, "It's so unfair that we have a Christmas tree at school and we don't have a menorah. I think it's unfair to Jewish kids." Michael was impressed by her progressive thought, particularly after having grown up in the Remington household.

"It's a Catholic college," her father said, shaken and clearly upset by his daughter's inclusive, liberal statement. "Why do they have to have a menorah?"

"And why does it have to be discussed right now when I'm here?" Michael said.

The table fell silent, except for Isaiah saying, "Shut up, Andrei."

So Michael decided at that point to stop seeing them altogether. When they left, Michael told Isaiah, "That is the last time I'll ever go to your father's house."

"I'm sorry," Isaiah said. And Michael stayed true to his word never to return to their home in Georgia. However, every time he encountered them in other ways, they stayed true to form.

One Saturday, Michael went to Washington, D.C., with

Isaiah and his family. On Sunday, they had to go to church. When they weren't with his family, Isaiah never attended mass. However, when they were with the family, it was expected that Isaiah and Michael would attend with them. "It was a miserable trip, the whole trip," Michael recalls. "It was a mass in honor of Cardinal O'Connor, who had just died, who was very homophobic. And we stayed through this horrible, terrible mass—long, long mass. And I remember at some point, I simply gave up and fell asleep.

"I fell asleep in the seat. And you have to get up and sit down, and get up and sit down. And I didn't get up at some point. So they bitched at me the whole trip, that I fell asleep in the church. I couldn't believe it. I went there with them, and I'm not religious, and these people were giving me grief because I didn't get up at some point. Why do they care? I'm an atheist. I'm not of their religion."

Just as Isaiah's family would never acknowledge the help Michael tried to give their son with the drug problem, they would not offer any thanks to Michael for at least attempting to get through their family event at this homophobic cardinal's mass.

"His family would have the most ridiculous conversations," Michael remembers of his experience with them. "Whenever they would sit down in a restaurant, the things they would talk about were like . . ."

"Oh, look at this nice curtain," one of them would say. "Aunt Fannie has one just like this in her house, remember? In her house in Connecticut?"

"No, no," another family member would disagree. "She has one with big flowers on the side."

". . . just conversations about *nothing*," Michael says. "His father's tirades about Bill Clinton, how much he hated Bill Clinton. It was the same tirade about how much he hated Bill Clinton over and over—embarrassing tirades. It was interesting to see an American Catholic family from

Georgia, a very typical one. But why did I have to watch it for three years? I will never understand."

When Michael involved Isaiah's family in his drug problem, Isaiah tried to act angry about it at first, but not too badly, and not for very long. "I think he did want everybody to know because he was really trying to get out of that," Michael says, clearly indicating that Isaiah was expressing cries for help in this way. "It was a bad addiction. And once I found the address of his drug dealer, and I went with a friend of mine who waited downstairs.

"It was a building in Midtown. They threw me the keys from upstairs, and I went in. It was a place where they were doing drugs, and because I was so crazy and tired of the situation at this point (I would never do it now), I went in and started going from one room to the other, yelling for him."

"Oh, Isaiah is a very nice gentleman," his dealer finally said. "No, he never stayed here. He always buys stuff and leaves. Very nice gentleman."

"Listen," Michael said to the dealer, "you sell him anything ever again, and you guys will be finished." Michael succeeded in scaring the dealers with his bravado, but knows with hindsight that they could have just shot him dead, right then and there. "Still, sometimes when I think about it, I can't believe that I did it.

"Drug addicts have a crazy imagination and the ability to lie. He would go to his psychiatrist, sit there with the shrink, and he would have drugs in his bag. And as soon as they were finished, he would go and do them. Drug addicts will betray you."

Isaiah's cousin, who had moved to New York a year earlier, feeling she knew better than Michael about how to handle a drug addict, moved Isaiah into her home. So he simply used drugs in his bedroom right next to his cousin's room. Of course, she found out, so her intervention lasted all of a week before she shipped him back to Michael. Again, never a thank-you was uttered by Isaiah's family for him dealing with his addiction essentially on his own.

"Why are you with him?" Isaiah's youngest sister one day asked. "Why don't you leave him? Why don't you throw him out? He's into some shit. I love him; he's my brother. But he's a jerk."

Michael appreciated his sister's sentiment, and got along better with her than with any of the others. This is perhaps why she is whom Michael turned to when things got out of control.

"I could get along with all of them if I wanted to swallow shit," Michael says. "But I just couldn't deal with that, so after a while I showed them that I wasn't going to do it anymore. I thought my relationship with them would get better once they found out what I was going through with him, but it actually didn't. It's not like we united to help him—not at all."

Eventually, Isaiah became physically abusive. At least, he attempted to be, but Michael was stronger than he was. He never was able to "beat up" on Michael, just because Michael was a stronger man. But through this, Isaiah's control issues—trying to have the upper hand in everything—and his hypocrisy were beginning to show.

After having Michael go through hell for pushing him in Puerto Rico, Isaiah had now taken to trying to hit Michael anytime something was going wrong. "You gave me so much grief about pushing you once in Puerto Rico," Michael said. "My God! Now it's all stupid to me how I reacted on that garbage of yours."

These kinds of control devices allowed Isaiah to keep Michael in a cage, to be on top all the time. He made Michael miserable, constantly apologetic, in fear that Isaiah would leave. It took Michael three years to realize that Isaiah was never going to leave.

Isaiah's abuse was not only physical, but emotional and verbal as well.

"If you call me that again," Michael warned after Isaiah had called him one of any colorful, anti-Semitic degradations, "you're gonna get the fuck out of my apartment."

He did it again, his tone full of spite. "Now what?"

"Now, you're gonna get your shit, and you're gonna get out of here."

Isaiah started gathering his things while Michael went into the other room with a book to read. While Isaiah gathered his belongings, he continued to beg Michael to reconsider. Michael kept his nose in the book, disregarding Isaiah's pleas. Isaiah took a long time to pack, hoping that Michael would cave in and stop him. "Goodbye, then," Isaiah finally said when he finished.

"Goodbye," Michael said. He tried hard not to show how nervous he was, wondering what he would do if Isaiah actually left.

"Okay, I'm leaving," Isaiah said, slowly walking to the door.

"Okay, goodbye," Michael said.

Isaiah closed the door behind him, leaving Michael alone in the apartment, his nervousness now turning to regret, even though he knew this was for the best.

A few minutes later, Isaiah returned, crying and begging for two hours, hoping Michael would reconsider and let him stay, asking Michael how he could let him go. If the situation were reversed, and Michael would have been the one groveling, Isaiah would have destroyed him. But Michael comforted Isaiah and took him back.

"Listen," Michael said. "I was really sorry you were leaving. I was hoping that you would stay." Michael shouldn't have been so forthcoming about what he was really feeling, but because of this situation, Michael had regained a little bit of the control Isaiah had stolen from him. "The whole thing was his being in control and being able to manipulate me," Michael says now. "And it was really, really difficult for him to see that it was over. At this point, he finally knew that if he's going to be rude and disgusting, I would kick him out—or at least let him go and not beg him to stay. So that was a big blow to him, and he cried about it for hours.

"But after that night, he cried a lot. He cried for many, many reasons. And he was not the macho man, in control, any longer. It changed everything.

"Sexually, it was very good. He went from being this guy who was always trying to take control over me sexually, and who had little sex drive (having sex about once a week), to having sex every day. He got into my sexual rhythm and ended up liking sex very much. He became such a perfect bottom, from being someone who was always trying to be a top with me, which he was not. But it was a control thing. He always tried that."

Although Michael took him back after the big crying game, the dynamic of the relationship had changed in such an irreversible way that it was only a matter of time before the two of them would finally part for good.

21

After three years of hell, the main reason that Michael's relationship with Isaiah finally fell apart was that Michael was finally in control. He knew Isaiah wasn't going to leave, and Michael had stopped trusting him.

"This life was not real," Michael says. "We had always planned to have kids. He always had wanted to have kids, and I just couldn't imagine having any kind of family or bringing up kids with someone so unstable and on drugs.

"Also, he was very antisocial. He had completely alienated every friend I had by being arrogant to them, and by dominating my time. He also had a very strange circle of friends. He had two girlfriends who were his girlfriends from school. And the only male friend he had was Father James, the priest from upstate, and that was it. That was all he had in his life. So it was just me, and his family. We would always go on vacations, just us. We didn't have any friends.

"But I had kept my friends. I kept in touch with them during the day. In the evenings, I spent all my time with Isaiah. Out of three years, two of those years, we spent every evening together—except for the nights he would stay out all night. I would not go anywhere without him. We were together all the time. I was actually a very good boyfriend to him, but it was just not a very healthy relationship."

Michael was finally understanding with 100 percent certainty a truth he could have simply read in any book: drug addicts are liars. "Drug addicts, no matter how much they love you, would betray you for drugs," Michael says he learned. "You can't trust them. Because being there for them, just comforting them, just enables them; they have no reason to quit. I didn't understand it.

"I don't know how he is right now, but it was the right thing for me for us to break up. He called me on drugs many times afterward, so I know he didn't stop for a while. But I know it was good for us to break up, because he never would have quit if we had stayed together."

Even though by the time the relationship had ended, Michael was basically just nursing a dying drug addict, he insists that part of the reason he stayed was because he was getting certain things from the relationship. "I was getting back whatever I could get back from a drug addict who loves you," Michael says. "I was getting his love, but it was the love of a man who is not stable morally, and who has a very strong mental drug addiction. So it was a delusion in some ways—just as it was a delusion to think Sevastian and I could have worked out because our embrace at the country house would have made a nice postcard—but I couldn't delude myself long enough that things would change.

"But he gave me a lot. He had impeccable taste—very good taste in terms of art, culture, in terms of films." Isaiah's main form of relaxation was watching films. On days off, he could spend the entire day in a cinema, seeing two or three movies at a time. At home, he was always watching smart, culturally stimulating films from independent directors or small studios. Even the comedies he watched were high-brow, thick with intellectual references.

"Drugs were something I was not familiar with, so I didn't understand it. I was covering his slow suicide, and I wasn't going to be helpful. I didn't know that. Now I know if someone is doing drugs, I step right away. I don't want to deal with that. I don't want to be near it. I know I can't help. A person has to hit rock bottom and then stand on his own. You can't help him; you can only cover the slow suicide. That's what I was doing."

Michael recognized with acute awareness that the drugs were slowly killing Isaiah. Although Isaiah did not die from his drug addiction, Michael understood that the outcome could very plausibly be death.

After their first trip to Moscow, they took another trip some months later to visit Michael's family again. Michael's mother, not one to mince words (which clearly runs in the family), said to him, "Andrei, he doesn't have any respect for you."

The second trip was very different than the first trip had been, but Lena was able to see through Isaiah's act enough to let her son know she was concerned. But Michael was given false hope from Isaiah because they didn't fight during the trip at all. He was behaving differently, and Lena liked him more than she had when she first met him. But Isaiah was impatient with her accent and stopped trying to communicate with her. "But she felt sorry for him," Michael remembers. "Because she already knew that he was a drug addict. I had told her. She didn't have strong feelings about him. They were not close, obviously. I don't know if she intimidated him, but he probably didn't feel very comfortable around my family.

"And his shyness is why he was never gaining new friends. I always had to explain him to people, because whenever people would meet him, they didn't like him. He never smiled. He was always looking for a boyfriend he could completely share his life with. He was never really looking for friends. He never had friends, and those he did have, he ended up breaking ties with them. He kept going back to old boyfriends, never trying to meet someone new."

The things that led up to the final day were all clearly pointing toward the end of the relationship, even as they were happening. Sometimes it takes hindsight to see the impending end to a relationship, but other times, the writing is on the wall. This was the case figuratively, and literally, with Michael and Isaiah's situation.

Because of Isaiah's control issues, Michael had stopped performing in his own movies for a couple of years—only writing, directing, and producing them. Isaiah wouldn't allow him to perform. "I did sacrifice that for him," Michael says. "But I would never do it again because it was stupid. Basically, I started appearing in the films again in 2000, just before we split. I had just decided he was not worth my sacrifice."

A week before the final day, Isaiah wrote Michael a sad poem. "It was a cheesy poem," Michael says. "But I thought it was nice of him. It was one of his ways to soften me, trying to keep me, some kind of act of desperation. But the poem was basically saying that it was me who had been nice, but who had suddenly turned bad.

"I think he understood everything. He understood how bad he was to me, and this relationship had no future because so many bad things had happened, that he had done to me, and that his family had done and said to me. He knew that I am what I am, that I was in New York City and meeting people, and that it would soon be over."

At about the same time that Isaiah wrote Michael the poem, Michael found out that Isaiah was seeing someone else. "It was probably the last straw for me," Michael says. But he feels that he found out about it because Isaiah stopped hiding it. "He realized we were going to break up, that I was going to leave."

When Michael had made the decision to break up with Isaiah, the situation had reached the point where Isaiah's drug addiction had worsened and he had gotten more violent. Isaiah had frequently written hurtful, threatening, anti-Semitic things on the walls in Michael's apartment. Later, he would paint over them out of remorse. However, in repetitive situations like these, there will inevitably come a day when the behavior is done one too many times.

DIE FUCKING KIKE was written on Michael's bedroom wall the day he finally asked Isaiah to leave. When Michael saw the scrawl on the wall, he telephoned Isaiah right away.

"We have to stop this relationship," Michael said. A sadness came over him because of the finality of his own tone. Isaiah recognized the tone as well.

The day before, Isaiah hadn't shown up at home again and he already was in a foul state. When he returned, he started arguing with Michael, going over all the reasons why Michael was the one at fault.

"This just isn't going anywhere," Michael said. "You know you're not going to change. My grandparents are arriving. I just don't have time for all that any longer."

"All right," Isaiah agreed, once again bluffing. "Let's just break up."

"Okay," Michael said. "That's what you want. I know it's what I want."

"Yes, that's what I want."

"Perfect. Let's just do it," Michael said. He left the apartment to blow off some steam. When he got back two hours later, Isaiah and his cousin were there moving things out—everything. "You really don't want to take all the stuff out of here. That's not how people do this. You broke into my apartment, and you're taking stuff out."

Unfortunately, as we see daily on *The Jerry Springer Show*, that is how people do this. Isaiah and his cousin continued taking things from the apartment. Michael called the police. Isaiah's friend, Father James, arrived just as the police got there.

"What's going on?" asked one of the officers.

"It's just domestic trouble," said the priest. "They're breaking up, and he's getting his stuff. It's fine."

"No, it's not fine because that's not his stuff," Michael said. "And I don't want someone to break into my apartment when I'm not here."

"Take it easy," said the officer. "If he lives here, he has the right to get his stuff out."

"Okay," Michael said. "He can get *his* stuff."

"Make sure he's only getting his things," said the officer. Then, to Isaiah, the officer added, "Sir, you have five minutes. You need to get your things and get out of here."

Five minutes later, the police made Isaiah and his cousin leave with what they had gotten from the apartment. "I understand," the priest said to Michael after the others had gone. "It's very tough."

"Yes, it's very tough," Michael said. "And I'm not really happy about your participation."

About a week later, the priest called and invited Michael to dinner. Michael agreed, because he was curious about what the man had to say. "I'm sorry. I really am sorry I was involved in all this," said the priest. "You don't remember me, do you?"

"No, what do you mean?" Michael asked, embarrassed for not knowing what he was talking about.

"I used to be a client of yours once. I came over to your apartment—probably three years ago—and we were talking about Russia."

Michael suddenly remembered having the priest as a client of his own. He remembered that the priest didn't think very sexually, that it had been very light sexual engagement with him. Father James contacted Michael a few more times after the breakup with Isaiah, but Michael wouldn't see him, and eventually the priest got the hint and stopped calling. Michael completely lost touch with Isaiah as well. "He tried to call me several times and tried to reach me, but I always refused to talk," Michael says. For a while, Michael continued to see Isaiah at shows when he would go to Broadway, but eventually that stopped altogether when Isaiah got the opportunity to move with his job back to Atlanta.

"He's a very strange character. He tried to date his first boyfriend, Rod, again, who is a good friend of mine now. We became very close friends after I broke up with Isaiah. Isaiah tried to accuse us of sleeping together, but it never happened. We never had sex. Isaiah tried to get back together with Rod, but it didn't work. Then he ended up dating and eventually getting back together with his second boyfriend, which is crazy.

"As always, he's basically going through all the same people in his life, trying to prove to each of us some kind of strange point that he can get people back.

"It was very difficult, and people ask me why I didn't break up with him for treating me so badly. The thing is, I was young. I loved him very much. I had moved to America because of him, and I had invested a lot into the relationship. That was all very, very difficult to just break and leave. I disliked myself for such a long time, and you can imagine I was angry with Isaiah.

"After you break up with someone like that, you realize this person kept you away from your work, from your friends. There were good parts about the relationship—his intelligence, his good eye for beautiful things, for culture— he brought a lot of culture into my life. He increased my love of art and musical theater, but at the same time, he kept me away from everything social that I liked. I'm a very social person. I like a lot of people. He kept me away from everything. It's not his fault, really. It was my fault for being with him. So I was angry that I had lost several years with him.

"Everything can be looked at from the point that it's good experience, but it didn't have to be such a long one. I was with a crazy guy for a long time. He was just a very complicated character. On one hand, he was a very handsome, highly educated, sweet and loving man. But there was another person in him as well, who was a horrible, cruel, rude, angry person who would be very violent. And you never knew which person would come up. So, you're always in a situation where you don't know when he'll change. And then there were the drugs, and you never know what night he'll come home.

"When you love someone like this, you're going crazy. How many nights did I not sleep because he wouldn't come home? Those nights, I would wait for him for a long time before I realized he wasn't coming. He wasn't answering the phone. So it was long nights because you know he's sitting alone in some hotel doing drugs. You think about things like, he could have a heart attack there and nobody would find him. They were horrible, sleepless nights. One night, his cousin spent the whole night with me, waiting for him. Another time, she told me I could call her anytime as soon as Isaiah showed up. But aside from that, I was basically alone, dealing with that.

"If I could turn back time, I would still do it, but not for three years. I would maybe do it for a year. I think I could learn the same lesson in a shorter time. I never had dealt with drugs in my entire life, so it was important to experience that and learn from it."

The breakup with Isaiah was one of the best things that ever happened to Michael. He realized at that point that

there had been a lot more bad things about the relationship than there had been good. He poured himself into his
company, working constantly to compensate for the way
he felt he had let Isaiah distract him from it.

Michael Lucas had set himself free upon the stage that
was New York City, ready to live again—possibly love
again, but it wasn't something he was looking for. "I've always enjoyed moments in my life when I was by myself,"
Michael insists. "But it was always too short. I'm not the
type of person who believes that everyone has to be in a
relationship. For good reasons, I'm always more produc-
tive without being in a relationship.

"It's very fashionable right now for gay people to be in
a relationship, and those who are not are in such desperation. It's crazy. There are friends of mine who I never see
because all they do is complain that they can't find a
boyfriend. It's very simple to find a boyfriend. Maybe people who are desperate to have a boyfriend and can never
find one, maybe there is something wrong with them.
Maybe their bar is too high. If everybody is looking for a
boyfriend and nobody can get one, that's strange. Because
everybody's looking. You're looking, and ten people on
your block are looking; a hundred people in the club where
you go are looking, and you can't find each other.

"It's the same with men and women. I think it's disgusting to think that women are born to make babies. Some
people love their work more than they love to be with
someone."

With his new freedom and his new lease on life and relationships, Michael nursed his fractured heart as much as
he could, knowing that the very next day, changes were on
the horizon that would be the beginning of the successful
life of the biggest gay porn star on the planet. His grandparents were moving to the United States from Russia.

PART FIVE

A New Dawn

One thousand forty-nine. That is the number of federal statutes that provide benefits, rights, and privileges to individuals who have the legal right to marry. I am at the end of my patience with gays who say they're not interested in obtaining the right to legally marry.

—Larry Kramer

22

Michael had been saving money from escorting and from his profits at Lucas Entertainment in order to get his green card and become legal in the United States. As soon as he got it, early in 2000 and just prior to his break-up with Isaiah, he made arrangements to begin moving his family to America. His green card enabled direct relatives to immigrate to the United States. His grandparents arrived in New York in September 2000, literally the day after Isaiah moved out of the apartment. Michael's parents and brother would eventually come several months later, in 2001.

"I had a very loving family, a very close family," Michael says. "And that includes my parents, my grandparents from my mother's side, and my brother. They all got their green cards. I moved them all here to live in Brooklyn, so now we're all together here. They love it here very much."

After the grandparents had arrived and got settled in, Michael took his company to his Russian homeland to film two movies, *To Moscow with Love* and *To Moscow with Love 2*. Along for the ride was Michael's friend (and fellow Isaiah ex), Rod Novoa.

Rod was no longer working in a restaurant by the time Michael and Isaiah broke up; he had become a fashion wardrobe stylist, dressing celebrities for a living. Rod provides wardrobe for functions like award shows, advertising campaigns, and television commercials.

"The way we became close friends," says Rod of Michael, "I guess after they broke up, one night I was out and Michael saw me at a club. I had just gotten back from Belgium or something. I was traveling. And I got back and he saw me. He told me what had happened with Isaiah, and that they had broken up."

"Let's hang out," Michael said. "Let's talk. I'd like to talk to you."

"From then on, we just became friends," Rod recalls. "He kept pursuing me to just hang with him. I guess he wanted a friend off from his relationship, to let go of some steam from the relationship. I was skeptical at first, but we ended up being best friends."

Rod, like Michael, reiterated that they have never been more than just good friends. "I think that's why we respect each other," Rod says. "Because, you know, Michael Lucas is a porn star, he's a New York celebrity. But between us, it's been a real friendship. It's not about sleeping with each other, which is great."

It is obvious with one glance at Michael that he does not dress like a stereotypical porn star. Of course, that's not surprising. Michael Lucas isn't stereotypical anything. He's always set his own standard and lives by his own rules. And he'll be the first to tell anyone that his biggest talent is to surround himself with the best people. Rod is included in that, and the way Michael dresses is taken directly from Rod's sense of style.

"I've always spent a lot of money on clothes," Michael says. "Things like Armani, which I still have in my closet from as far back as 1995. Usually, clothes are not a good investment, but when my muscles got bigger, some of my pieces became too small for me. I ended up selling them for more money than I bought them for. That was always the way I was choosing my clothes. I was making the right choices. Nothing I ever bought was a waste. I never threw anything away, except, of course, things like sneakers, underwear, socks, or training pants. Everything else—every suit, every jacket, every coat—whatever I've bought and whatever I buy now, is always with the thought that it could be a collector's piece.

"I am also very careful with my clothes. I never give any-thing to dry clean, except coats and suits, never any sweaters. I separate and hand wash them—well, now I have a lady who does that for me. And my closet is like a room. I have the whole room for a closet. If I don't feel like wearing some-thing because it doesn't fit, I sell it and get more money.

"These are the kinds of things that porn stars don't usu-ally do. Lots of porn stars spend a lot of money on drugs, on drinking, on partying, on bad clothes, but they are wasting their money. I do invest a lot of money in clothes. But now it's a very small part of what I invest compared to what I make. It was never a huge part, but it was always a priority."

Having a friend who is a fashion insider like Rod helps when making those choices, too. But it's really at Michael's core to place importance on how he looks. His mother says when he was little, she would always put him in clothes that he could ruin because she knew that five minutes after he went out in them, they would be covered in dirt. But she also remembers the day that changed, when Michael came up to her with ruined clothes and said, "What's this about?!"

Since they became good friends, Rod has been his right-hand man in terms of Michael's always looking his best. In fact, he can think of only one time—relatively recently—

when Michael had just gotten back from a trip to Tel Aviv. Michael had gone directly to the office from the airport and called Rod right away.

"Rod, my clothes and hair are a mess. I'm absolutely beat."

"Why don't you take a little time and hit the salon?" Rod suggested.

"I'm just so tired," Michael said. "You know, this is the first time in years I don't care what I look like."

It must have been one hell of an exhausting trip to make Michael say that. That one situation was the very rare exception to the rule of how Michael Lucas appears to the world. Which is why, when he took his crew to Moscow to shoot the films, Rod was right there.

But it wasn't just a work thing. Michael also took a new friend of his, whom he had met that year at the GayVN (Gay Video News) Awards. Michael was in town for the awards and needed a date. A friend of his suggested that he take an actor friend of his, Gerald McCullouch. Being apart from Isaiah, Michael made friends with people quickly, and he was completely in his element with Rod and Gerald accompanying him to Russia. For them, it was their first time in Russia. So Michael actually got the chance to show off his homeland to people who cared. Michael, a self-proclaimed people person, was desperate for friends after having been sequestered for three years. While he was developing close friendships with Rod and Gerald, he also kept in touch with his childhood friends, Ivanna and Anna. But the more the merrier, as they say, and Michael was really seeking out people he could be close with.

It was December 2000. Michael and Isaiah had been broken up for three months. Michael called a friend of his, Elias, at about seven or eight in the evening and said, "You always tell me you're going to take me to parties and that you know all these people. But you've never taken me to a party."

"Well, I'm at a party now," Elias said. "Would you like to come?"

"Yes!" Michael answered, his haste as unbound as his spirit.

"Well, actually this party is nearly over."

"That's okay," Michael said. "I'm only ten minutes away from where you are. So, I'll come."

On his way to the party, within minutes, Elias called Michael back to dissuade him once more. "Andrei, it's nearly over. Why don't you forget it?"

"I'm already here," Michael said, standing on the sidewalk in front of the building. He approached the doorman, who asked him if he was with the party. "Yes," Michael said confidently. "Seventh floor."

When Michael got to the party, he realized that his friend had lied. The party was just getting started. Elias had been trying to date the host of the party and didn't want the competition of Michael Lucas to be around to cock-block him. Elias started saying things to Michael like, "Hitler was not that bad after all, because at least he built the Autobahn." He bragged about hating Republicans, all the while confessing that he hadn't voted for Gore because of Lieberman. Eventually, Michael discovered that Elias used drugs and, true to his word to never be around them again, cut all ties with Elias.

However, Michael was having an incredible time at the party. He met the host, Richard Winger, who was a businessman and president of the board at the New York City Lesbian, Gay, Bisexual & Transgender Community Center. Michael found Richard to be a nice man, but one surrounded by 160 friends. So he didn't have the opportunity to really talk to him.

The next day, Michael called Elias to get Richard's telephone number. "I would like to call and say thank you very much for this beautiful party," Michael said. "It was a really great party, great people. The food and catering were incredible."

"I cannot give you his number without permission," Elias said.

So Michael called Information and asked for Richard's number. It was not unlisted, so they readily gave the number, and Michael called to thank him.

"Richard, this is Michael from last night," Michael said. "I would like to invite you to dinner to thank you for the party. Would you have dinner with me?"

The next day, Michael and Richard met for dinner. "We had a great time," Michael says. "We had a very nice dinner. Then we went to his apartment and had very good sex—*very, very good sex!* He's very sexually open-minded, and he enjoys having sex for a long time, everything that I like. He likes fucking; he likes everything. He's often into different things, which is great."

The next day, Ivanna, Michael's oldest, dearest friend, came to New York for a visit. It would have been difficult to believe, when seeing Michael at this time—his grandparents living in Brooklyn, his parents and brother on the way, his childhood friend visiting him in New York, and a date or two under his belt with an incredibly sexy, interesting man—that only three months before, he was ending a three-year relationship with an abusive drug addict. Things were changing fast, and Michael was ready.

Although Ivanna hadn't seen Michael in a long time, they had kept in touch. So for her, he was the same Andrei he had always been. "The only change that happened to Andrei is the physical change," she says. "When he was growing up, he was a regular-looking guy, nothing out of the ordinary. After I saw him in New York, having not

seen him in a couple of years, I just realized that he became a really handsome man. He is an extremely handsome man now, and he wasn't like that when he was
growing up. But on a personal level, he is the same Andrei
I grew up with. He is the same sweet guy."

He got the opportunity to introduce Ivanna to Richard
before Richard left New York for South Africa for a vacation the day after Ivanna arrived. When Richard got to
South Africa, he called Michael right away to say, "I miss
you."

"I miss you, too. I can't wait until you get back,"
Michael said. "How is South Africa?"

Richard told Michael about South Africa, and would
continue to do so, as they talked almost every day Richard
was gone. However, Michael had other issues brewing at
home. He needed to take care of Ivanna, who had just left
a long, bad relationship in Germany, much the way that
Michael and Isaiah had ended theirs so recently. He and
Ivanna began to commiserate about evil men, and the two
of them began to get closer and closer.

23

The chill that hung in the New York winter air that December wasn't the only thing pushing Michael and Ivanna into each other's arms. They had both been in unhappy, abusive relationships that they basically had to escape from. They were both lonely, and they had loved each other for a very long time.

"He went to law school," Ivanna says. "I'm a technical person; I went to engineering school. So we were separate for a time, but we always had kept in touch. And I would say that after moving to the United States, I think we became closer because we were going through similar experiences—moving to a different country, getting acclimated—it's a culture shock. So we grew closer. And we're still very close."

Michael had mentioned to Ivanna that he had been in magazines, and over the years had continued telling her about what he was doing in terms of his career. But until she actually came to New York and saw him, she hadn't really comprehended the scope of his success. "I was shocked for a moment when I found out he was a rising star in the porn industry," Ivanna says. "But then I realized that he was experiencing an extremely successful career, and I just respect it. He's always had my respect, and now even more. It's not even fair to say that I was shocked. I wasn't. I was surprised, but I wasn't shocked, and I totally accepted it right away. He has a lot to be proud of."

Michael was no longer the shy, inexperienced boy from Russia who was afraid to touch another person. Now he was Michael Lucas, famous for having sex, for being good-looking, for having a killer body. In Michael's apartment, on a cold December night while the two of them sat talking, the wind outside made its way through the busy lit streets and the dangerous dark alleys alike. The city outside buzzed with current, while inside, a calm assurance came over Michael as he leaned in to kiss Ivanna.

"Come on," she whispered. "You're gay. What's going on here?"

But Michael had always loved her, and he pressed on. "I do love her still, very, very much," Michael says. "She's the only woman I ever loved. It was a very strong emotional level of love for her." Ivanna gave in to her mutual strong feelings for Michael and made love to him, wrapped in the warmth of his arms, while outside in the city, the snow had begun to fall.

Michael and Ivanna fell asleep in each other's arms that night. The snow came down in buckets—large flakes, rich with detail, wafted down from the sky to rest upon the streets of Manhattan. For the next three or four hours, millions more large flakes slowly descended. In the early hours of morning, when the sun's light just below the horizon began turning the sky from its saturated pitch into the deep purple hue of the approaching dawn, the large flakes gave way to a smaller, faster lot. Another couple of hours, in which these tiny crystals of chill barreled down, sealed the previously pristine flakes in a tightly packed protective layer. When the sun rose, the snow glittered brilliantly along the New York City skyline.

Michael and Ivanna awoke to the first day of the new

year, 2001. Wrapped in blankets, they started the day by
walking to the window together. They pulled back the curtains, revealing the West Village spread out before them,
covered in bright white snow. Children were already bundled in snowsuits, coats, and hats, throwing snowballs and
gathering large mounds of snow to display a neighborhood
street full of snowmen. People were skiing in the streets.
Even through the glass that separated the chill outside from
the warmth in the apartment, Michael and Ivanna could
hear the children's shouts below, could see their joy.

After breakfast, Ivanna stayed at the apartment while
Michael went to play squash with his friend, John. John
won almost every match against Michael, but they were
friends. Michael enjoyed spending the time with John, and
the game was fun even if he knew he most likely wouldn't
win. Out of ten matches, Michael might win two of them.
But on this day, Michael won the first game, the second . . .
. . . the third!

"What the fuck is going on?" John asked.

"This is *great!*" Michael laughed.

After Michael won the sixth match in a row, John was
unsettled. "What are you doing?" he asked Michael. "You've
been smelling your hand all day."

"Smell my hand," Michael said, offering it to John.

"What the fuck *is* that?" John asked after he smelled
Michael's hand, then batted it away.

"You know Ivanna?"

"Yes . . . ?"

"We had sex, and she was having her period."

John was about to throw up. "What the hell are you
doing?"

Michael ended up winning all ten matches against John
that day. "It was like I had wings," Michael recalls. "Ivanna
and I had so much sex, sex all the time. We went everywhere holding hands, confusing everybody in New York.

All my friends were totally shocked. But that's how much I loved her.

"I just couldn't stop smelling my hand all day. She had her period, and it wouldn't stop me from eating her out; I loved it so much. All my friends were confused."

"What, are you trying to be straight now?" they asked.

"No," Michael assured them. "I'm gay."

Every night, Michael went out to gay clubs with Ivanna on his arm. And every night, the two of them were making love. Yet nearly every day, Michael was talking to Richard, the host from the party he had gone to, who was on vacation in South Africa.

"Is New York all gay?" Ivanna asked one night after they left yet another gay club.

"Well, actually no," Michael said. "If you go out, there are gay people, but there are many more straight clubs than there are gay clubs. Don't judge it by West Chelsea. Aren't you having a good time?"

"Of course," she said sincerely. "I'm having a wonderful time."

But their emotions from years of platonic love were entering into all the sex they were having. Ivanna was menstruating, so her hormones were raging, and confusion was setting in. The next night, at another gay club, Michael started flirting with a man at the bar. Ivanna saw what was going on and started crying. True, her hormones were making it worse, but she was falling in love with Michael in a different way, and what he was doing was genuinely hurting her.

"Listen," Michael said, feeling like a selfish idiot, "I'm really sorry. Let's get out of here." Once outside the noise of the club, bundled together against the chill on the quiet street, Michael continued, "I didn't mean to do that to you."

"No," Ivanna said, letting reality seep back in. "It just

reminded me of my boyfriend from Germany who was cheating on me."

"I'm so sorry."

"It's not you," Ivanna assured him. "I love you. I've always loved you; you know that."

"I love you, too."

"Let's just keep things the way they are," Ivanna said. "I'm here for one more week, right? Let's just move on."

The next seven days were like a fairy tale for Michael and Ivanna. They made love, went to Central Park, toured New York, and got each other back on track from the horrible relationships they had endured, somewhat parallel, for the past three years. Until one morning, Michael and Ivanna got up, he drove her to the airport, and she was gone.

How is it possible for someone like Michael Lucas to be so in love with a woman, make love to her, *enjoy* making love to her in ways some straight men don't, yet still claim to be gay? Michael's first porn film experience in Germany had been a straight porn. He had also slept with women in college, his affair with Galina, for example. How can this kind of man be gay?

In *Gender Trouble: Feminism and the Subversion of Identity*, Judith Butler states, "The taboo against incest and, implicitly, against homosexuality is a repressive injunction which presumes an original desire localized in the notion of 'dispositions,' which suffers a repression of an originally homosexual libidinal directionality and produces the displaced phenomenon of heterosexual desire." Butler's argument makes sense, particularly considering the way so many repressed gay youth try so hard to be straight, they think they can talk themselves into it.

We often oversimplify the phenomenon Butler discusses with the term "experimentation." As in Michael's case just before he left Russia, many gay youth will identify as bisexual prior to eventually coming out as being totally gay. Many of these people may continue sleeping with members of the opposite sex for years before finally realizing the attraction is not truly there.

This kind of repression can also be found at the core of "therapies" that attempt to change a person's sexuality based on "religion." The people who emerge from these programs and say they've changed their sexuality haven't really done so at all. They've only succeeded in repression (which will be talked about more later in terms of Freud's discourse on repression). This repression, as Butler indicates, can create an illusion of heterosexuality. However, a person's true feelings will always eventually reemerge. And in the case of "ex-gay therapies," it is often after attempted marriages and births of children. The pain this causes for these attempted families could entirely be prevented if only people could accept themselves for who they are to begin with.

Michael realized this that night at the club. "I would never marry Ivanna because I don't want to destroy her life," he says. "I'm a gay man. I don't identify as bisexual. It's not about who you can fuck. I enjoy people who have a gay mentality. I enjoy the company of gay men. I love gay men, and I am loved by gay men. It is my life, and my life is not a family life with a woman and having a sick, boring, straight life. I know I will always want to have sex with men, and she deserves better."

This is not to say that Michael's love for Ivanna is diminished in any way. The two of them have always loved each other and always will, and it is because they love each other that they know they cannot be together as a couple.

24

Richard returned from South Africa and Michael began seeing him on a regular basis.

"I have a really busy schedule," Richard said upon his return. "Because I'm president of the board, I have a lot of responsibility. But I'd like you to be included, as long as it's not boring to you."

On the contrary, it was just the catalyst Michael needed in order to become more involved politically with the gay community. "So I went to many dinners with his friends," Michael remembers. "I met his circle, who were all these people who were involved in charity. His work was about involving people to donate money to the New York City Lesbian, Gay, Bisexual & Transgender Community Center. So, I started going with him to board meetings, and I attended several of them.

"I was very surprised the first time I saw him at a board meeting. He really didn't care how he dressed. He was wearing a sweater that was probably fifteen years old. And I liked that about him. He was nice, very sweet, very funny, very intelligent.

"He was also very open-minded. He was always supportive of my business and was always interested to listen to me talk about it. Although he's not into porn and was never the type to sit and watch it.

"I felt protected with Richard. He was there at a time when I had ended the relationship with Isaiah in which I didn't feel protected and had gone into having to protect myself. With Richard, and with his friends, I felt protected, and that's very important to me."

By Valentine's Day, Richard had begun referring to Michael as his "boyfriend-in-training." After a few months, Richard asked Michael to move in with him. Michael knew already that he loved Richard, but had learned from his haste in the past that he should give the relationship a little bit more time first. It was because he loved Richard, and wanted the relationship to work, that he wanted to do it right.

By the time the fall had arrived, Michael finally agreed to move in with Richard. He continued to keep his apartment in the West Village, which also served as an office, for a few more months. But under a few conditions, he conceded and moved in with Richard.

"He smokes," Michael says of Richard. "But not much; only about three to five cigarettes a day. We agreed, since I don't like to be around smoke, that he would only smoke on the second floor of the apartment—never downstairs where the bedrooms are. Also, I didn't like the way he was dressed. So I took him shopping and dressed him the way I wanted him to be dressed. I took him to Armani and Donna Karan, stores that were proper for a man of forty-six, which is how old he was at the time. He liked it, and we actually live very happily together.

"He travels a lot, often to South America. His term as president of the board is now over, and he concentrates a lot of his energy on his father's business. His father died about eight years ago, and left his whole manufacturing

business in South America, which produces flatware, to
Richard. So he spends a lot of time in South America. His
brother lives in Australia; his sister lives in London. And I
work a lot and travel for business, so it's not like we spend
every second together, which I think is very healthy for a
relationship."

Michael and Richard have tapped into what could be
one of the healthiest secrets to a lasting relationship—that
they should enhance each other's lives, not *become* each
other's lives. While interested in each other's work, they
still maintain their individuality, which has enabled them
to be successful on their own as well as being a couple. For
many couples, this is easier said than done, but for Michael
and Richard, it works like clockwork.

"I need a lot of space," Michael says. "What I like
about Richard is that he has no problem entertaining himself. He has no problem going to see a movie by himself if
I'm busy. He has no problem reading books for hours. He
reads constantly, whatever comes out. If it is getting any
decent reviews, he reads it. And we see all the operas at the
Metropolitan Opera that come out. We go to exhibitions.
And we travel together a lot—we just came back from Argentina; before that, we went to Italy. Our next trip, we're
going to Peru, so we travel for fun a lot."

Because of Richard's position with the New York City
Lesbian, Gay, Bisexual & Transgender Community Center, for ten years he was one of the top fund-raisers for the
GLBT community. This is one of the things Michael loves
so much about Richard. "He basically made it possible for
the Community Center to function," Michael boasts. "And
to have their doors open for hundreds of gay groups. He is
doing an amazing job, and I think the gay people of New
York City should build a monument to him while he is
alive. He's done a lot for the gay community of New York

City, and is a man I respect so much. There are not many people like that, who are doing good things just for the idea, and it's very, very good of him."

Michael's respect for Richard's altruism is apparent in the way the tone of his voice changes when he begins talking about the things Richard has done for GLBT people in New York. And Richard himself gives a humble "thank you" when he hears that the work he has done in New York is felt across the nation, either directly or indirectly, and is appreciated by all of us.

"I think as my business picked up, I became more involved in activism," Michael says. "I think that Richard was always a good example for me. It happened all at the same time; I got rid of Isaiah, met Richard, and I could concentrate entirely on my business. Then, of course, Richard was so devoted to the cause. He really is the one who was interested in making the Community Center work. He truly is a great guy. He's not there because of his ego. He's there because he's interested in making it work."

Richard was raised in a quiet home, where family members never raised their voices during conflict. Michael was raised in a Russian Jewish home, where loud talk (within conflict or without) was standard fare. So things in the Lucas/Winger household may not always be handled with seamless simpatico, but there is always respect.

"He is very liberal, as you can imagine," Michael says of Richard. "He has a lot of respect for what I do, and is very supportive. Lots of relationships lack the respect. We have mutual respect for each other, and that's one of the most important things. He is probably the best thing that ever happened to me in my life. So, in terms of finding the right person to be with, he is probably the best thing to ever happen. I'm very much in love with him, and he is definitely in love with my life, that's for sure. I've never had such a good time with a partner as I've had with him, my husband."

The world and time had opened wide up after Michael broke his ties to Isaiah. He felt a renewed interest in life, love, his career, and the people and culture that have shaped his life. Great film directors like Fellini and Visconti who influenced Michael culturally, friends like opera costume designer Alexandre Vassiliev, have all had a lasting impact on Michael in a way that sets him apart as a person—not just as a porn star and producer.

25

When Michael's parents and brother finally moved to America in 2001, joining him and his grandparents here, they were forced to sell the country house that Michael, and three generations before him, had grown up in.

"I don't miss Russia at all," Michael says of his oppressive homeland. "I never want to go there. I don't miss the apartments or anything else. But the country house, which I associate with my childhood memories, I miss very much. It's very disturbing. I can't live with the fact that they sold it. I have dreams on a weekly basis about the house.

"My memories of the country house are so strong. I had a dream that woke me up last night, that I went and the people who had bought the house weren't there. And I was worried that they could come in at any second and find me there. I cannot make peace with the fact that there are strangers living in the house that belongs to me and my great-grandparents. There were many generations of my family there."

The people who bought the Treyvas country house said it was very sad to see Michael's parents leave the house for the last time. "Your parents are very strong people," they said to Michael. "I know they were very sad. But they just—when the deal was done and they gave us the keys, they just turned around and went to the car. They never looked back. But we saw the pain in their eyes."

"It's very difficult to leave something when you have it for generations," Michael says. "Very difficult. But that was three years ago. Back then I couldn't tell my parents not to sell the house. They sold it for $50,000, and I couldn't give them that much money for it then. Now it probably costs more because prices went up in Russia. But three years ago, $50,000 was a lot of money. I regret not being able to give them the money."

Michael goes back to Russia to visit sometimes, but finds it very difficult to go to the country house. "I want to, but I don't want to," he says. "Because I feel like I'm going to cry when I'm there. That's what happens in my dreams all the time, that I'm walking into the garden and I start crying. And I don't want that. It's tough for me.

"It's not complicated for people to understand that I don't miss Russia. It's more complicated to explain how I miss my childhood and the country house where my family lived together, something that is dear to my heart. It has nothing to do with liking Russia. I miss my family living together, being a kid, when I didn't have to think about things you have to think about when you're an adult."

But the selling of the country house was not the only thing to put a damper on the joy of Michael's parents moving to America. Michael says that one of his biggest regrets in his life is not convincing his parents to move sooner, so that they could have found out sooner about his mother's cancer diagnosis.

When Mr. Bregman, Michael's paternal grandfather, died of cancer, Michael hadn't seemed to be affected because they hadn't been very close. However, the thought of losing his mother—the very heart of his closely knit family—has been devastating to him.

As soon as Lena arrived in America, she was diagnosed with cervical cancer. "I don't talk about this to anyone," Michael says of this incredibly private matter. "When you tell people something like that, they try to give you these checkup calls. And you know, what do you get from that? You bring it up at the dinner party or anywhere, and you put everybody down, and everyone feels that they're obligated to talk to you about it. I don't want to be a downer, so I keep it to myself. But it's a very big tragedy in my family because she's very young, and it's very hard to find the right words because there's nothing you can really do. It's out of your hands."

When the doctors first told Lena that she had cancer, she was devastated and literally petrified with fear. For an entire week, Lena stayed in bed, sick with worry about her condition and what the prognosis would be. She cried several times a day, holding Michael's hand, when all he could do was be there and give her his strength.

"My family has always been a big part of my life," Michael says. "They were my backbone. Suddenly, it's shaking. That's what pisses me off, incredibly, not being able to do things. It drives me crazy that I can't fix it, I can't make any decisions, cannot find the right words." Now, although Michael has always done so much for his family, whenever he does something for Lena, she worries that he's doing it because she's sick. "I just have to be very careful," Michael says. "If I ask her if she wants to go to Italy on vacation with my father, she feels like it's her last trip or something. What can I do? It's just very tough."

But everything Michael does is a significant help for his family, whether he realizes it or not. He finds it very difficult to talk about, and won't even turn to Richard for help. Michael is very averse to people showing emotion for him; it makes him uncomfortable. On the outside, he seems to think that showing emotion is unnecessary, because it doesn't help anything. The result is that he truly is appearing strong for his family, which helps them a great deal. However, the concern is that burying feelings that come up in situations like this can later result in devastating breakdowns.

So, after the diagnosis, when Lena was consumed by her fear, Michael was there for her. "They will operate," he said. "And everything will be fine."

Lena attempted to let Michael convince her that what he said was true, but it still took time for the news to settle with her.

"Do you remember the hell you were giving me about touching myself when you thought I was masturbating?" Michael asked, trying to make her laugh. It worked. They both laughed—Lena through her tears, and Michael as he gripped his mother's hand.

"You know, we didn't know anything about those things. That is what we were taught, and we just didn't have any information," she said with lighthearted explanation. "You were such a shy boy, Andrei."

"I remember," said Michael.

"Everyone used to tell me they didn't know how you would ever be able to take your clothes off in front of girls. You were so very shy." She laughed telling him the story, knowing now that there was never much danger in his staying too shy. But the nostalgic conversation was enough to get Lena away from her tears and to realize that there could still be good things to come, that nothing is ever so serious that you can't look back on it one day and realize you've been lucky in so many ways.

26

With Isaiah in the past, and a promising future with Richard ahead of him, Michael was finally able to begin building his business the way he intended. One of the ways he was able to begin really building a name for himself after laying the solid groundwork he was able to achieve in spite of Isaiah, was with Fire Island.

Fire Island is a resort off the coast of New York that has historically been a gay retreat for several decades. Made famous through early films, Fire Island drew the attention of gay men across the United States and throughout the world. However, many who hadn't seen the handful of films produced there, either in whole or in part, were unaware of the island. Michael Lucas's porn project there was a quid pro quo that helped put Lucas Entertainment and Fire Island on the map at the same time.

"Fire Island is a very challenging thing to produce," Michael says. "People don't film there because it's very expensive to bring all the equipment, models, and crew, and to rent a house there is very expensive. A lot of people didn't know what Fire Island was before I started doing the movies." It helps then, if your rich new boyfriend already owns a house on the island. "That's how it started," Michael says.

"The second reason would be because nobody has filmed there since the 1970s," Michael continues. "I think there was only one movie ever produced there, so it is another niche which is not used. The island is very famous because it's a huge gay community. It's a New York vacation spot where everybody goes, from famous designers, to politicians and actors, and it's a very world-known gay resort."

More than one nonporn film has been produced on Fire Island, such as *Boys in the Band* and *Longtime Companion*, but none of them have brought it the attention that Lucas's series has in terms of being a free-for-all gay resort. The island itself is beautiful, and no cars are allowed. The island is very narrow, with a bay on one end and an ocean on the other. The private properties are very large, and the natural settings have been painstakingly preserved, creating a stunning combination of ocean, trees and birds, and luxurious spaces for vacationing and relaxing.

"It's such a beautiful island that's so close to the city," Michael says of his inspiration to film there. "And since I have a house there and spent time there, I decided it would be a beautiful place to film. The funny thing is, the problem filming there is that you have to bring all the equipment, crew, and models, and accommodate them."

Fire Island is becoming older with time. New owners of the resorts there have spent a lot of time publicizing the resort to a younger market, but its exclusivity can be expensive. Not many young people can afford to go there. However, the seniors who reside on the island or who own property there often refuse to rent their properties to Michael for shooting his films.

"Those seniors who collect money from producers who film documentaries about Fire Island are complaining that there is no fresh meat on Fire Island, that it is all older people on the island now," Michael says. "They don't understand that their best promoter is Michael Lucas. *Fire Island Cruising* is the best promotion. It's the illusion that I give about this place, because I bring ten or twenty hot guys in the month of June or July, then everybody thinks that Fire Island is not a bunch of old millionaires, that instead it's a bunch of young guys fucking their brains out."

However, when Michael asks those same property owners if he can use their house for filming, they either ask for thousands of dollars, or they flatly refuse because they don't want their house used for porn production even though the films promote the island in a way that would bring the young gay men that they want there. "A PR company was hired by the owners of The Pavilion to promote Fire Island," Michael says. "Any PR company will not do five percent of what I will do with distributing tens of thousands of *Fire Island Cruising* movies. How many of them were rented, and how many used for video streaming? Hundreds of thousands of people saw *Fire Island Cruising* movies and have the illusion that it's a hot, sexy place and that they should go there. So they should put a monument to me on Fire Island, but they are way too arrogant for that."

Ironically, it is the minority straight population of Fire Island who has been the most accommodating to Michael for filming there. The same is also true of his filming in New York. "I very often communicate much better with straight people than with gay people," says Michael. "Some gay people are more conservative and close-minded and arrogant and prudish than straight people. A lot of straight people are much more open-minded." Even people Michael is friendly with tell him he can't film in their home, that they can't expose their house to porn.

"It is ridiculous," Michael feels. "Their property values are going up with me advertising the island. As long as the place is considered hot, their properties are more expensive. I make this whole island a hot place, and this is something they don't appreciate."

Resorts who hire PR companies to promote the island are failing to realize the benefit that could come from paying Michael to advertise their properties in trailers on the *Fire Island Cruising* series, but Michael hasn't even approached them about such a venture. "These self-hating homosexuals are way too arrogant," he says. "That's what I have to deal with on Fire Island."

The lack of cooperation with the gay locals aside, Michael Lucas's *Fire Island Cruising* series has become a staple of Lucas Entertainment's repertoire, and the most successful series to his credit. Currently with an astounding eight films in the series and more in production, Michael Lucas will continue raging against the dying of the light to produce the series that has helped make Lucas Entertainment a gay-household name.

Fire Island Cruising	2000
Fire Island Cruising 2	2001
Fire Island Cruising 3	2002
Fire Island Cruising 4	2002
Fire Island Cruising 5	2003
Fire Island Cruising 6	2004
Fire Island Cruising 7	2005
Fire Island Cruising 8	2006

27

Just as Michael had wrapped his head and heart around his family and his business, he did the same thing with his friends. Gerald McCullouch, the actor Michael had met as his date for the GayVN Awards, and whom he had taken to Moscow with Rod when he went there for filming, had become a very close friend to Michael. Gerald, who has appeared in hit television series like *Beverly Hills 90210*, *Melrose Place*, and more recently in his recurring role as Bobby Dawson on *CSI: Crime Scene Investigation*, says that he and Michael got really close, really quickly. Gerald is the life of the party and tends to be the little red guy on Michael's left shoulder.

"I had come to New York before we were going to Russia," Gerald says. "And we had planned one night in New York to go out before we left, just to go have dinner, hang out, go club-hopping. I think we may have been going to the opera that night; I'm not sure. I came to his apartment in the Village."

Gerald interjects that back then, "In my heyday, when I was quite the hellion, I used to be quite a connoisseur of making really good pot butter. If you eat a pot cookie, or a pot brownie, it stays in your system for a very long time because your body is always digesting the THC, but it doesn't taste very good. It's like you're bringing someone a nice brownie and you dropped it in the dirt and say, 'Well here you go, try it anyway.'

"So I brought it over to Andrei and—I think it was maybe the first time I had seen his apartment. We were just sitting around talking, and I said, 'Hey, are you ready for a night?' "

"Yes," he said. "I'm ready."

"I brought you something."

"What did you bring me?" Michael asked.

"I brought you a pot cookie," Gerald said, not knowing really how to gauge the language barrier at that point. So Michael just assumed that this happened to be what the cookie was called. He didn't make the connection. "It tastes horrible," Gerald added.

"No, it tastes great," Michael said, eating the cookie and trying to be polite. From Michael's point of view, he thought that Gerald was just some new friend, or fan, who had baked him a cookie. How pathetic, Michael thought. Here is this little actor from Los Angeles coming and bringing me a cookie that tastes horrible.

"It's gross," Gerald insisted, laughing. "Drink some milk with it or something."

"No, it tastes great."

"No, it doesn't. It's a pot cookie."

"Well, this kind of cookie is great."

"Awwhhh, Andrei," Gerald said, still laughing.

"The night moves on, and we had gone out to dinner," Gerald says. "And we were at some straight bar up in Midtown. And I started getting a little high, and I think Andrei had, too. And it was funny because we were sitting on this ledge, on this step up, that people in the club couldn't see. And people would trip going up the steps. So Andrei and I, sitting over by that step, kept watching people trip as they went up. And he and I just started falling out laughing—literally. We had tears coming out of our eyes for about thirty minutes."

At one point, Michael stopped and said to Gerald, through his own laughter, "I don't know what's wrong. I don't feel that good."

"It's the pot cookie," Gerald said, also still laughing.

"What do you mean? The pot cookie?"

"Andrei, you ate a pot cookie."

"What do you mean?"

"Pot. Marijuana," Gerald said. "The cookie had marijuana in it."

"But I don't do drugs," Michael insisted.

"Well, you just ate a pot cookie."

"No," Michael said, his panic rising.

"And then he just freaked out," Gerald says. "Here's this guy coming in from L.A., getting him stoned for the first and only time in his life. But until the point when he freaked out, I don't think I've ever laughed that hard with anybody that incessantly. We were on the ground laughing. Just sheer laughter like that with somebody is very rare. It's one of my favorite memories."

Then, on the day they were leaving, they met up with Rod and the cast and crew who were going, and they left for Russia. Gerald and Rod both remember the trip fondly. "After Michael and I first met, we maintained pretty close ties via phone and e-mail," Gerald says. "I had a lot of respect for him initially because his family means a lot to him. And he kind of challenged that stereotype I had in my mind of what a porn star would be. And I thought he was a really great human being. We can have really great political conversations, and I really respected that.

"I travel a lot with my career, and I was heading to New York for a period of time for some meetings, and he said that he was going to Russia, and invited me to go with him. I met his family there, just before he was planning to move them all to America. And we went to St. Petersburg, and he shot a movie while we were there, which was a trip. And I think during that time, it just—our friendship, being in Russia together, seeing him in his country, and meeting his family—it was just a great opportunity, not only to see a whole different culture than America, but to see it in that way. And Andrei treated us really well when we were over there, and he's just a sweetheart. He opened up his home, and his family. That I really respected."

In addition to his friendships with Rod and Gerald, Michael also was keeping in touch with his friends from his childhood. Obviously, he has stayed in close contact with Ivanna. And although not *quite* as closely, he has also stayed in touch with Anna. When she moved to America, she (like Ivanna) didn't feel that he had changed much at all. "He got more self-esteem," Anna observed. "In some ways, he always had it. I wouldn't say he had really changed a lot. He got more patient in many ways. The main thing that was the same is that he could always get what he wanted. And he always knows what he wants. For as long as I've known him, he's always known what he wants. It's amazing to talk to a teenager and have them already know what they want. He always knew. And I think it's very unusual."

Michael's growing circle of friends, all of whom he became very close to, was something he needed so much. He had been kept away from having any kind of a social life when he was with Isaiah. Now that he was with an emotionally healthy, loving man like Richard, he was able to pursue friendships with people he considers very dear. Through another friend, Michael met a television journalist named Jason Bellini, from CNN.

Jason was intrigued by Michael's career, but was apprehensive at first about what it would mean for him to become friends with a porn star. He was concerned about the stigma. However, Michael soon broke down the stereotypes Jason harbored regarding his career. Now Jason is thankful to have Michael for a friend and appreciates everything Michael has contributed to his life.

"Michael is a really decent person whom I could have good conversations with, and who very quickly became interested in helping me," says Jason. "How could Michael Lucas, the porn star, help me, a CNN correspondent? And what would I admit to him helping me with? Well, he helped me with things like my clothing, my hair, and with the makeup I would wear on the air—all the things that I never paid that much attention to because I considered myself a journalist who didn't need to be concerned with all of this.

"I was concerned about my appearance, but I wasn't obsessed with it. I guess I was more like a straight guy in that respect. It was an inconvenience and a nuisance to have to deal with it. But he wanted to help me craft a look.

"And he called up people right then and there. He called his stylist friend, Rod Novoa, and set me up an appointment. He set me up an appointment with his hairstylist, Frederick Fekkai, who gave me the best haircut I've ever had in my life. When I went to work the next day, it was compliments everywhere I went down the hall on my new haircut. He was giving me the Michael Lucas makeover, and people were impressed.

"People at work were saying, 'That's a really nice jacket. Where did you get that?' He helped me out a lot. He took an interest in me in an area that he saw as a bit of weakness, to get a bit of style in my life. So I never told my colleagues that I'm getting a makeover from a porn star, Michael Lucas. But that was the reality of the situation."

Just like it was with Gerald and Rod, Michael and Jason quickly became friends. Michael was always interested in what Jason was doing, or what he had to say. The two of them discussed politics and books. "Those are the types of conversations we would have," Jason says. "And he would look at some of my reports as well, and he offered me critiques of my reports—the way I looked on air, the way I conducted myself on air, my mannerisms. And he was harsh—he was Michael Lucas harsh—but he was also right. And so he pointed out some things to me that I needed to improve upon, and I listened to him. All the while, I kept thinking, 'I can't believe I'm getting professional advice from Michael Lucas, a porn star whose video is at the XXX store around the corner. What will people think?' "

28

To help promote Lucas Entertainment, part of Michael's job is to visit different cities across the country. "Once a month, I travel for publicity, but it's not like I'm touring," Michael says. "I don't care how much they pay me. I care about how much people come and how much publicity I get. It's all publicity for my company. They usually pay about $1,000, which is okay—cash, you know. That's fine with me, but I would never go for the money. I mean, I take the money, but I go because after I visit certain cities in certain states, we have lots of new customers and big boosts of sales.

"Plus, I like to travel. I never regret that I went to places like Omaha, Nebraska. I mean, there's nothing wrong with knowing how bad it is. I've been there. I saw it. I would never go again. I wanted to see it. You know, you appreciate what you have when you see how bad it can be. It's a place without a face—corn fields and corn-fed people—it's absolutely terrible. Everybody in the gay club was so drunk. They couldn't walk or talk; they were saying nonsense. I was looking at them, the way they were dressed, and that was the most embarrassing thing. They were oversmoking and drinking tons of liquor.

"After that, you come to New York, and you're like, 'Thank God. I'm surrounded by normal people.' But I go to places like that and entertain the people who don't come to New York, who are born, live, work, and die in Nebraska wearing ugly clothes, working on the ugly street, reading the disgusting newspaper. There was a huge gay club there for gay people who look like they're straight—no individuality. But also, there are pretty cities where I would never live as well. But I have no problem traveling there.

"I've also been to Eastern Europe, Russia, and South America. I love to travel to South America. Jason, Richard, and I are going to Argentina, and we'll have a marvelous time. We're staying at the Four Seasons Hotel. It's a country that is very beautiful. It's very European, as far as I know; it's very interesting. It has a great museum, great scenery, and I'm very much looking forward to it. I went to Brazil—not for publicity, just for vacation, although I did perform while I was in Brazil. I performed in Israel as well. I have an amazing time traveling and performing. It's a great way to meet fans and to make friends and connections.

"For my trip to Israel, I stayed for ten days, and I have several friends whom I now am quite close to because they travel to New York all the time. Same as in Hamburg—I performed in Hamburg. Everybody who lives in Hamburg has a house somewhere else, so they also travel all over the world. Incidentally, Hamburg is a very cosmopolitan city. So I have friends in Hamburg and friends in Brazil. I have friends everywhere; it's great. It makes you a citizen of the world, where you can feel comfortable everywhere."

Although Michael loves to travel and values the people he meets wherever he goes, nothing can compare to the love affair he has going with his home—New York City. For the man who has traveled all over the world and seen beautiful, old cities in the four corners of the earth, New York City is the only place he can call home. "I miss New York after one week, wherever I am," Michael says. "It usually happens after a week; I'm totally ready to go back.

"The whole world is incredibly nationalistic. Take France, take Italy, Germany—these are very nationalistic countries. I mean, Paris is quite metropolitan, but compared to New York, it's nothing. In Europe, I never felt at home. In New York, I felt at home from the very beginning. Everybody who is multitalented, who is energetic, who is anything, they're all here.

"A lot of people say they like Europeans. If you like Europeans, move to New York, there are tons of them here. If you like South Americans, you don't have to move to South America; move to New York. It's such an incredible city; I wouldn't live anywhere else. There are cool cities like Los Angeles, but I wouldn't live there because I like New York's street energy. Los Angeles has zero street energy."

For all the publicity he can do in the United States and abroad, his home and business are planted firmly in New York City. He built his business around New York City, when everyone else in the industry was filming on the West Coast. His family is there; his husband is there. Most of his friends are there, and there is never a dull moment in New York City, particularly for the biggest porn star in America.

Certain facets of Michael's relationships suggest that Michael has friendships and relationships only with people who can assist him in some way or further his social or career status. Even Michael's closest friends have commented on the unique "relationship" or "arrangement" that he has with his partner, Richard Winger.

Another example that could lend itself to such a deduction of his character could be the exchange that occurred when Michael met Boy George, formerly of the eighties supergroup Culture Club. Their meeting at a club in New York resulted in the following message from Boy George to Michael in the first of a series of e-mails between the two of them.

The e-mail to Michael stated that Boy George was interested in dressing Michael in his clothing for a private photo shoot as well as privately filming Michael in a pornographic setting. The e-mail flattered Michael and suggested that a trade be arranged for Michael's participation in the private session. Boy George offered to let Michael use some of his music in one of Michael's films for free in exchange for posing for the photographs and the filming. "Oh, that boy," George said in conclusion, referring to the person he was with the night they met, "was boring but he liked having his ass eaten and he left his underwear as he rushed out sober and possibly horrified. Who knows."

Does Michael knowing people like Boy George further his social status in New York? Does it give him credibility to hobnob with the likes of these celebrities and make deals with them under the radar? If a quid pro quo actually went on between Michael and Boy George for music in exchange for some private shootings, that may or may not increase Michael Lucas's stock on the P-list ("P" for porn, of course), but Michael did interview Boy George on camera for his Web site and Boy George's music did appear in Michael's movie *Manhattan Heat*.

Michael Lucas never has a problem saying what he thinks about anyone he comes into contact with. Anyone who puts himself in the line of his fire, particularly in a sexual situation, should really just brace himself and take what's coming to him. Michael controls his world with an iron fist and a razor-sharp tongue. But there is one situation that continues to tie his hands and silence him, leaving him alone and wondering what to do.

When Lena, his mother, was diagnosed with cancer, the doctors operated on her cervix to remove the disease. A year later, in 2002, during a follow-up visit that would enable the doctors to make sure there were no other areas of concern, they determined that Lena's cancer had metastasized. Again, with the diagnosis, she spent a week in bed, crying to Michael and holding his supportive hand. The cancer was now on her lung.

Lena went through another operation to try to remove the cancer. She came out of the surgery very well; then she underwent chemotherapy. The family hoped that, this time, her suffering would finally be over so that she could get on with her life.

29

As Lena was finishing her last round of chemotherapy in late 2003, Ivanna phoned to tell Michael that she was getting married and would be having a baby. "It is great for her," Michael says of Ivanna's relationship now. "She found a guy. He loves her, and they have a baby. She is my age—half a year older—so it was time for her to have a baby. That's what she always wanted.

"When she told me she was getting married, though, I felt pain for a moment. I'm happy for her. But at the same time, it was painful for a moment when she told me because, it's like, it's gone now. But it's the way it should be. I mean, what kind of life—I'm a gay porn star—what kind of sick life would that be?

"Again, there are too many things. Yes, I love her. So what? Yes, we can have great sex, but so what? There are a lot of other things. It's not a Fellini movie; it's real life. It's my life, and she wouldn't want to have a life that mimics a crazy Fellini movie. She needs a husband who will come home every day, who will love her, who will love their kid, and who will live their straight life. And I can't be that. I'm *so* not that. But I always did love her, and I think I always will."

Life goes on, as they say. People get sick, and they get treated. Old friends become lovers, who move on and have babies. Running concurrently with the life we live and the relationships we have is the work that we do and how we manage ourselves in it. Michael Lucas has proven repeatedly that he always gets what he wants. And although he is not able to control his mother's condition or the frustration a gay man feels when the woman in his life moves on to marry a straight man, he has always controlled his business. He hauls out that iron fist and that razor-sharp tongue and marches on.

Michael went into his doctor's office one day and came face-to-face with his early American past from 1997. Karim, the dear, sweet man who had written him a bad check seven years earlier, sat across from him in the waiting room.

"Hey," Michael said loudly, "you owe me something from 1997. Aren't you Karim?"

"Yes," he said. "I'm Karim." He had been working for a major magazine in New York. But now Michael had his green card and was no longer an "illegal immigrant."

"Well, one click of my finger, and I will make you famous overnight," Michael said calmly. It's so easy to be calm when you clearly have your boot on someone's neck. "Do you really want to fuck with me?" Karim knew who Michael was, that he had become successful, and that he meant business.

Michael pulled out Karim's check, which had been on file for seven years. The next day, he received all the money by messenger. "Plus, for every year, I told him to pay nine percent on top of the amount," Michael says. "And I got it all. I knew back in 1997 that the situation was very unpleasant, but that I would eventually get paid the money. Everything I wanted to get, I always got, and it's only a question of time. I don't let things go. I am very honest and hardworking, and sometimes people would say

I'm a bitch. I'm sure Karim will call me a bitch from now on, but that's okay, because I did what I needed to do. And I did what was right."

It is impossible to find anyone who is successful who hasn't been called a bitch. "You have to be tough," Michael says. "You have to be ambitious. It's a very simple target when you're dealing with a tourist who doesn't have any rights in this country. But you always have to look into the future. You always have to know that things can change, and you never know who will become what. And you better not fuck people over and mess with people, because sometimes people mess with you back, and with good reason. So I don't mind being called a bitch."

Michael Lucas puts the "business" in "porn business." He has always been, first and foremost, a businessman. When he was a child negotiating theater tickets, he was a businessman. When he was a law student running his own tourism company, he was a businessman. When he was an escort prostituting himself on the streets of Eastern Europe and America, he was a businessman.

"I've been very open-minded since the beginning; that's how I got to know Michael," says Rod Novoa. "But I've gotten even more open-minded. I've become more open-minded about the porn industry. I work in his films sometimes, doing wardrobe. So I can see how hard, literally how hard, all the people involved in the film production and all the actors—how hard they work. So it's really made me see the industry in a very different way, to the point that I respect the industry very much. Because when you're working with Michael—and I can only speak for Michael and his company—it's a serious business."

It is Michael's business ethic that has thrust him to the top of this competitive, highly saturated industry, and has put his face on the cover of dozens of magazines—both porn and mainstream, nonporn publications. It's why in

2004, his business had expanded at such a rate, his company relaunched its Web site, LucasEntertainment.com, to include features and user interfaces that had never been available before. "We update it every day from our office," Michael says of the new site. "People can go to the Web site and contact me for any reason—if they want to be an actor, if they want to communicate with me through the forum page, the discussion. It's a great Web site."

But an even better way to communicate with Michael, and see who or what is on his A-list or his shit-list, is to visit his blog every day. LucasBlog.com is the most real-time, comprehensive way to peek into the mind and mouth of America's bitch-of-a-businessman porn star. People can also access the Web site with a paid membership and download any movie he has ever produced. This state-of-the-art approach to porn has secured Michael's position as the leader in his industry.

However, there was still one area of Michael's life that Michael could not beat with his quick wit or all the powerful connections he had anywhere in the world.

30

Eventually, the doctors told Michael, Lena, and the family that the cancer had returned. "We cannot do anything more because the operations have been useless," said the doctor. "We'll just have to watch you, and hope." But Lena and the family all know the statistics. There is only a 19 percent chance of survival after five years of having lung cancer. She can live four months, five months—she might live a year. No one knows.

Michael's emotions and actions regarding this family tragedy really show his generous, loyal character. Everything he's done since he left Russia was to make it where he and his family could live in America together. Then, he continued working to make sure they live the best life possible—with advantages, travel, and the ability to live in freedom. His friends, those who call him Andrei, respect him the most for the way he treats his family.

Although it is difficult for him to discuss, Michael shares how he feels about how devastating it is facing his mother's terminal illness. "It's very difficult because it's only me and my brother," he says. "And he has no patience for my mother or for anybody at this point. He finds it very irritating.

"There's only a thirty percent chance that chemotherapy would improve anything at this point, so they would just kill her with chemotherapy if they were to try it again. So we decided not to do it right now. My brother can't deal with it at all. So it all falls on me, my father, and my grandparents. It is difficult to find the words when there is nothing to say. You can't say it's going to get better, because that's not so. And we're not religious, so I can't use religion as a way out because I really don't believe in that.

"This is probably the first time in my life when I'm in a situation where I'm so powerless, and I really can't do anything. At the same time, I know I have to go on with my life. And I have to smile.

"I do take Celexa to keep the depression away, because I have to be strong for my family. I always take my family to the opera and to the theater. This week, they're going to see three different plays. But it's very tough.

"I have a very big family, which is what I'm used to— my grandparents, my parents, and my brother. But my grandparents are eighty-five years old, and my mother is really sick. My father's family all died from cancer, so I don't know what's going to happen to him. I really don't know if he will be able to go on without my mother. They've been together for thirty-two years, and he can't imagine being without her. So today I have a big family, but tomorrow I might be all alone. That's a very depressing thought, because they are the people who loved me like nobody else. It's kind of terrifying that I will lose the only people who really care.

"I have lots of friends, but I have to get used to the reality that the people who really love me unconditionally will be gone soon. It's made me realize I'm not very close to my brother. We are so different. Maybe it will change, but I really am kind of mad at him right now for not wanting to deal with our mother's problems. He's going to be twenty-three, and he doesn't get the scale of it. He doesn't want to understand.

"Part of it is denial, I know. But he just came for a visit for three days, and I didn't even know him. My mother would burst into tears and say, 'I can't live. I don't want to die. Isn't there anything anybody can do?' And he just got angry and said, 'You've got to stop it,' and walked out of the room. I was kind of amazed by his behavior, and I said, 'Listen, you will one day realize what you said, and you will always feel guilty.'

"He left America seven months ago because a friend of his in Russia offered him a management job in his company. He's making tons of money, which he wouldn't be able to make in America in the short term. He's very wealthy, and he's not helping our parents at all. He really doesn't. He lives in my parents' apartment in Moscow. It's very disappointing for me that he's my brother, yet he's not there for the family. He much more cares about the girl-friend he just met.

"He's had this girlfriend for four months, who is blond and has long legs. He was running around New York looking for jewelry for her and asking my mother if she knows a good store to buy jewels. So that really, really disgusts me. 'How are you asking our mother that? Why don't you buy her something? You're going to lose your mother, and you're going to lose your grandparents sometime, probably soon.'

"When my mother goes, it will probably shorten the life of my grandparents as well. And I don't know if my father will be able to keep going without her. I really am concerned. And my brother—I'm sure I will forgive him, but I'm not sure what kind of relationship we will have afterward. We are so different. He's embracing everything I hate.

"He lives in Moscow and loves it. It is the capital of a nationalistic empire. There's no place there for diversity, for foreigners, for anything. We are too different; he only cares about money. I like money, like everybody else. But it's very difficult for someone like me, who grew up surrounded by his family, suddenly to realize that this part of my life and my youth, it will be gone. I talk to them every day of my life. No matter where I am, which country, at least once I will talk to my mother and at least once with my grandparents.

"My brother is not doing that. He calls my parents; it's not that he's horrible. He calls them once a week, or once every two weeks. But he's not as close to them as I am. It's nothing like that. Even when he was here and was staying with my parents, he was all the time on the phone or on the computer. He wasn't really there, you know? He was physically there, but he wasn't there.

"I said, 'Our grandparents irritate you, but they're eighty-five years old!' And he has no patience for that. They ask him, 'How are you doing? How is your company?' And even that irritates him, because he's not interested in talking to them. But it's like, have some patience. They're old. Maybe he will change dramatically, but for him, it will be too late.

"I didn't really have anyone to advise me. So he should really listen to me. Because I know that you have to show gratitude and you have to appreciate them, because nobody will love you as much as your family. For him, it's a little different. He's a straight guy. He will have his family. For him, it's going to be easy. For me, I don't think it will be that easy. I'm not sure if I will have kids and a family. Today, I have a boyfriend, and that's really good. But I don't know how it will all go in the future. Nobody knows."

Michael seems to keep hoping for the best from his brother. But he is correct about the fact that his brother will have a lot to regret once he's lost everyone. Even if he's not as close to them as Michael is, it's still going to hit him hard. It's possible that Pavel, Michael's brother, is dis-

tancing himself as a protection device. But it's only going
to end up hurting him more later when he realizes how
much he's missed out on. Michael made another good point,
that Pavel has the advantage of having an older brother.
This is another part of his family that he should be thankful for right now. How sad that he just really doesn't understand.

And how sad that Michael understands all too well.

"It's part of life," Michael says of his mother's illness.
"Many people go through it, and now I have to go through
it. But I think she is holding incredibly well. She was in
bed for three days after the doctors told her the final prognosis. But now I think she's adapting to her situation. It takes
time, but then you live in fear of her pain that will start one
day. If you're ninety years old and dying, you can say you'll
get better. When you have terminal cancer, you cannot say
you'll get better. You can only say you hope it won't grow
very fast. Let's hope there will be a miracle and it will stop
growing.

"That's what I'm saying. Let's try to enjoy every day. It
will be hard on everybody. You have to find the strength to
get out of depression.

"With such a small percentage of a chance that chemotherapy would work, she could still die in a year. So you
can just go on living your life, or you can take chemotherapy and throw up every day and spend every day in bed.
So do you really want to spoil the last year, or whatever, of
your life?

"Very tough decisions.

"It's ridiculous that they can't treat lung cancer. They
can already treat HIV and AIDS, but they can't treat lung
cancer. It's ridiculous. I think there should be more money
for research. There should be something done about that.
Cancer is such a killer, and it's terrible for everybody. They're
torturing people with chemotherapy, by putting lots of

poison in the person. And they're watching to see if the poison will kill the cancer cells. But you're killing the person, too, with this poison.

"Now they're doing some research that can help the body fight, but it's in such little numbers. They're only treating a hundred patients with it. There might only be thirty or forty percent success, and if it doesn't kill it, it will just slow it down. People are having to wait two years to get this treatment, but there's nothing special about these numbers. I've read everything there is about this vaccine, and it's just not good enough.

"So many people died from cancer last year—so many. I have friends with parents who have cancer, and they're watching them die because they're going through this chemotherapy or that operation. They spend the last years of their life in misery. Most of them that I've talked to say now that they would never let them go through the chemotherapy, if they could turn back time.

"I'm just happy that I'm in a position to make things more comfortable for her. I wish she would have more years to live, so I could do even more with them. I wish that I could do more. But of course, I'm happy that I'm able to send them to Philadelphia and Italy. They go to all the concerts and to the opera. I take them to all the nice restaurants, and it's great that they can do it. I'm thankful, at least, that she's not in Russia and wouldn't be alive anymore. Here, there is a hospital, at least.

"And I wish I could do more . . ."

31

Building a business takes more than just saving money and reinvesting it. It takes more than long hours and a work ethic. It takes plain street savvy, and knowing where to invest your time and with whom to invest your time. Even Michael's biggest stars at Lucas Entertainment have been high maintenance, but Michael sees early on who is worth the work and who is not.

"Porn stars are always complaining," Michael says, "and they're very insecure. I was not in touch with porn stars until I got some exclusive models. And once I got some exclusive models, you have to be in touch with them, right? And when you're in touch with them, you're kind of terrified by how needy they are, how insecure they are, how desperate they are. How *irresponsible* they are. It is just incredible."

Michael's exclusive, Wilfried Knight, agreed outside of his contract to do a film for Lucas Kazan (whose movies Michael distributes). Michael called him on it, and Knight had to explain to Michael that the part was a small one and that since he already agreed to do it, it was too short notice to back out. "No worry," said Wilfried. "Your money is not going down the drain. [I have] no plan to go elsewhere at all, I respect you as my boss and friend."

In a later e-mail, Knight confirmed Michael's assessment of his insecurities by saying, "Thanks again for trusting me and coping with the insecurities I sometimes bring with me." Knight goes on to assure Michael that he intends to remain an exclusive to Lucas Entertainment, or that if he works for another company, that it would be under the advice of Michael himself. However, Knight persists that he expects to work on a regular and ongoing basis. Just as Boy George did, Knight interjects flattery toward Michael in an attempt to tame the beast that is Michael Lucas's rowdy, erratic temper. Knight's conclusion is less flattery, however, and is more the general consensus of those who have worked under Michael's direction. He states that he wouldn't want to do porn under any other circumstances than the environment that Michael provides.

But for this attention, Michael expects complete loyalty in return. Michael says he gets e-mails from Wilfried two or three times a week asking for money or something else. Things like, "Could you please put a hundred dollars on my account today by four?" when it is already three in the afternoon. Other e-mails or calls might have him saying, "Can you pay for my hotel, because I've come to New York to escort and I don't have money," or "Loan me five dollars to eat."

Once Michael took Wilfried to a Broadway show. Before the show, Michael had to rush to the hospital because his mother had an appointment with the doctor. The appointment was a very difficult, three-hour affair because her treatment was going nowhere. It had been a very difficult day for Michael, to see his mother crying, as well as his father and grandparents.

After the appointment, Michael had another appoint-

ment to get his hair cut at eight, then to see the show with
Wilfried at nine-thirty. Michael's dog was in his office because he had asked the guys in the office to take care of
him during the day. He called Wilfried and said, "Wilfried,
do you have my keys from the office?" Michael had given
him the keys so he could check his e-mail throughout the
day. "Could you please pick up my dog and bring her at
nine before we go to the show?"

"I'm sorry," Wilfried said. "I'm meeting a friend for
dinner right now."

"Okay," Michael said. "It's only two blocks away. After
dinner, before you come over, could you grab her?"

"I didn't take the office keys from my hotel room."

"Okay," Michael said. "Don't worry about it."

After he got off the phone, Michael thought, "You little
piece of shit. I am doing everything for you, and you give
me excuses. Instead of saying, 'Thank God I can do something for Michael Lucas now,' he's telling me he can't." So
Michael called him back and left him a message saying,
"You know what? You can give me the keys back from the
office and check your e-mails from the Internet café. And
don't ask me to help you. If you can't even help me go pick
up the dog."

Wilfried left dinner and went to pick up the dog. The
next day, they apologized to each other. Michael perceived
the incident as a betrayal. While this is a minor example, a
situation Michael had with his model Kent Larson was
similar, but on a grander scale.

"I was a little bit involved with Kent Larson at one
point," Michael recalls. "And I helped him. I guaranteed
his apartment. He's not my exclusive, but he came on my
set and he was doing a very good job. He was in a bad situation in his life, and was going through some big problems. I listened to these problems, and you shouldn't listen

to porn stars complaining to you, because then they will complain more. It actually wouldn't be a good thing to do, to help them."

At the time, Larson was living in Dallas, Texas, and couldn't find a place to live. Michael signed for the apartment for him. Several months later, Larson e-mailed Michael saying that he couldn't afford to pay the rent on the apartment. In a return e-mail, Michael said, "You know what? I came to this country with nothing. I had to pay for my green card—tons of money to get it, and nobody helped me. I never asked anyone for help. You are six-foot-four, fucking huge 250 pounds of man, thirty-one or thirty-two years old, and you cannot pay $1,000 a month for your apartment?

"You know why?" Michael continued. "Because you are a piss-off. You are just a waste of time; you are a loser. That's why." After that, Michael felt he had lost his money and a friend because the friend forgot that Michael Lucas had helped him. He only remembered that Michael called him a loser when he couldn't pay his rent. Michael had even bought his bed because Larson told him he was sleeping on the floor.

"I will never, ever do something like that for anybody else in the porn business because then you hope they will take their life in their own hands, but they don't. They go and party."

The payoff is that people like Wilfried Knight and Kent Larson give Michael what he needs most. The only thing they can possibly give him. Good porn. They possess what it takes to be porn stars, and Michael Lucas pays for it personally and financially.

32

Michael Lucas is always looking for a star, and doesn't have many exclusives. When he's thinking about exclusives, and whom he wants to hire, there are many requirements. He's always looking for who he can make big, as big as he became. That is important for him, because his company cannot be successful if it's all about Michael Lucas.

Michael is always looking for fresh faces, and he always explains to men, besides having great looks, in order to reach something, they both have to work on it. They have to have a very strong desire to become a star, and a lot of patience.

"Unfortunately there is a lack of patience and discipline," says Michael.

MICHAEL LUCAS'S TEN RULES FOR BEING A PORN STAR

RULE 1: You Have to Have the Look
"Whenever I look for a star, it always starts with the physical—with looks. And that has to be a combination. If you want to be a big adult star, you have to have a hot face, hot body, and a nice size of dick. You don't have to have a humongous dick, though it's always a plus. But it has to be something over seven inches, and nicely shaped."

RULE 2: You Must Love Sex
"You have to like sex and be uninhibited, and enjoy sex in all its forms."

RULE 3: You Have to Want it More Than Anything
"These can actually go in any order, because one without the other wouldn't work. You've got to have a strong desire to get to the top and remain on top. You have to want to reach success and completely concentrate on your career. Once you've made up your mind, you don't go back. You don't go into retirement. You don't compromise your work because of relationships with people who are trying to manipulate you. And again, discipline. That's the most important thing. Because it's very easy to get into the business, to make a few movies and even sometimes to become a star. What is difficult is to remain on top for many years."

Michael has been in the business over ten years now, and he's getting bigger and bigger, and getting more publicity. To do that, you have to be incredibly disciplined and have a strong desire for that.

RULE 4: Love Yourself Tremendously
"Forget about ever partying and doing drugs, and it's best not to drink. Be in control. Invest in your health and in your body. Love yourself tremendously. Take care of yourself. Be in the gym every day. From the time you do your first movie, and until you do your last movie, get in better shape and better shape, and better shape. You always have to be very lean. You go from very lean, to leanest. From three-pack of abs to six- or eight-pack of abs. You always surprise them with your appearance. You never disappoint them because they will never forgive you."

Mario Ortiz, not an exclusive, but certainly a regular

face in the films of Michael Lucas, agrees with the importance of staying off drugs. "I am drug-free also. I'm not
ashamed to admit it; I used to use crystal, but five days ago
I celebrated ten months sober. The camera doesn't cover
anything; it shows everything. If you look at scenes, you
can tell the difference between somebody high and somebody sober." Ortiz also says that it's difficult to work on a
set where people are using drugs. "You know they can't
control themselves in the moment, and you have to work
for you and for them also. I've had to talk to the director
and say, 'I cannot work with this guy because he cannot
control himself.'"

RULE 5: Have a Strong Presence
"You always make your presence stronger and more ef-
fective."

RULE 6: Avoid Overexposure
"Never make a hundred movies. In order to be a star,
you can make just twenty, but they should be great performances, one better than another, with confidence and hot
sex. Working for every company, and appearing in a hundred movies a year, that's overexposure. You have to be
choosy. Work for good productions and good directors.
And you have to look great in every production, and they
cannot make you look great on their own."

Mario Ortiz says that Michael Lucas is the master at
making models look great. "The thing I like about him is
that he's in front of the camera, so he knows what it's like.
He demands a lot. He's really a perfectionist, so he likes
you to look perfect in front of the camera, so he always re-
minds you to tighten your stomach or put your butt higher,
things like that. He always cares about those kinds of things
that make you look good, which is very important. I respect him."

RULE 7: Be Flexible
"You should be very versatile in terms of one day you're dominant, and in another movie you're very romantic. You should appeal to many different audiences. Have your hair longer or shorter, your body more lean, or more muscular or buffed."

RULE 8: Have a Strong Personality
Similar to Rule 5, Michael says, "You've also got to have your personality."

RULE 9: Know How to Promote Yourself
"You've got to be intelligent and know how to give interviews. Have a good public relations person or company. I always take great care of my models with top photographers and top publicity. I never use porn photographers; I use fashion photographers. That's one of the keys to my success. My photography is the best in the world of adult gay porn because I use only very highly qualified fashion photographers. That makes it much more interesting. IMAGE—You have to be exciting to journalists, to publicists, to your fans."

RULE 10: It's All in the Attitude
"You have to have a great attitude, a very positive attitude for people to want to work with you."

With all these tips, you might make it, or you might not. But if you don't do these things, your chances of making it in the porn business are much slimmer. It is a lot of hard work. Michael says he hasn't met many men who are this committed. "Wilfried Knight is incredibly committed, and I can think about maybe one or two others," Michael says. "But as far as today, it's me and the second one would be Wilfried Knight. I have a lot of hot guys, but it's difficult to be on top. It's difficult to get on top, because guys also get old very fast and burn out. Sleepless nights, escorting all night long. You have to know when to turn your phone off and go to sleep. You have to know when to party, when to sleep. Otherwise you won't last long and you will start to look bad."

For Michael, total commitment comes on the set and off the set. It's very important to have that total commitment to your career as an adult star. You must consider everything, such as grooming, clothes, showing up for the awards show, or even going to a business dinner or to the club, you must behave properly. "You can never be drunk," Michael says. "Don't dress like a cliché porn star in a see-through broken T-shirt with pierced nipples. Be dressed in a beautiful suit. Everyone saw your body already in the movie. Now go and put yourself in a glamorous suit like Gucci or Armani. That's what makes a model interesting."

33

In addition to his work with the GLBT community, Richard, Michael's husband, also sponsors the Metropolitan Opera. So, it stands to reason that he and Michael are there relatively frequently. They get the opportunity to see everything that comes out. Michael has seen some operas ten to twenty times in his life, especially his favorites like *La Traviata* or *Carmen*. When Michael travels, he likes to see operas outside New York as well, and so he has become very familiar with different opera houses of the world, and he has had the chance to meet several opera divas.

In fact, whenever he sees an opera diva, he makes it a point to go over, introduce himself, and talk to her. Recently, while out dining with Richard, they caught sight of Deborah Voigt.

"Let's go say hello," Michael suggested to Richard.

"No," he whispered.

"Why not?" Michael asked. "I think she'll say hello and be happy that we came over."

"No, she's a big opera diva. You know, we shouldn't disturb her."

"No," Michael insisted. "You see, divas are like porn actors. They have very small audiences. Their only audience is people who go to operas. The same with porn stars. Their only audience is gay people who watch porn. Gay porn and opera audiences are shrinking so much, so the trouble with opera divas is that they're seen on stage in full makeup and costume. When it's all gone, people don't really recognize them. If someone recognizes an opera diva, it's someone who is an opera fan and who can recognize them without the clothes, and have the guts to come over. They probably don't get it once a month. Trust me; she'll appreciate it."

Richard reluctantly agreed, and as usual, Michael was correct. They approached Deborah Voigt and told her they were big fans, and she talked to them for half an hour. The same thing happened with Olga Borodina, Renée Fleming, and with several others. "Probably, my most interesting conversation was with Olga Borodina," says Michael. "And after that I actually said to myself that sometimes it's better not to know the person you adore than to know them, because you lose the magic.

"Because Olga Borodina is a big soprano, probably one of the five biggest, and she was so vulgar. It was just the opposite of what I had imagined. It made me realize that opera divas, like ballet dancers and people in sports, their talent just happens to be their voice, or their ability to dance. They are not the art; they are the artist. They are the instrument."

This is the very point that Oscar Wilde makes in his Preface to *The Picture of Dorian Gray*. It is a discourse about how, to properly criticize art, you must first separate the artist from the art. There is value in studying art that way, because if someone is biased for or against an artist, it will easily sway their opinion of the art. For example, Ayn Rand was a venomous, drooling homophobe. I would hate her work before I even read it because I hate her politics. Whereas, if I didn't know a piece I was reading was hers, I might like it until I found out who had written it.

Conversely, if a porn film has been produced by Michael
Lucas, I automatically know I'm going to like it, simply because I'm familiar with his style, and I know he produces
good work. However, if I were to see a scene that I didn't
know he had produced, if it featured a model I don't care
for, I might not like the scene without knowing that Michael
Lucas had produced it.

So there certainly is value in separating the art from the
artist, for both the sake of the art and for the sake of the
artist. However, it can't be the only way to see either. Eventually, it all should be taken into consideration in order to
get a complete, fully informed opinion of a piece of art—
whether it's gay porn, poetry, or opera. It is interesting,
though, for Michael to have echoed the sentiments of Oscar
Wilde so dead on.

But he clearly has legitimate reasons for agreeing with
Wilde. "I was shocked when I would see ballet dancers on
stage. It's wonderful, and it's so rich and beautiful," Michael
says. "And you talk to him and realize this person is absolutely dumb. He's so primitive and stupid. It's what I
would expect from someone who runs up to a bull.

"I find that actors are much more interesting. They are
much more educated. They read; usually they are smart. I
think it's because if you are a stupid person, you wouldn't
be able to act unless you are in the hands of a great director—like maybe Nicole Kidman. I think she is quite a dumb
woman. I never met her, but when she gives interviews, she
doesn't come off very bright. But people I know like Rupert Everett, they are incredibly bright. They are very interesting, very intelligent.

"It's funny. A lot of people will recognize me in the opera
because of a Web site that's up for gay opera fans. And as
a gay opera fan, someone referred me there. There was a
very serious discussion posted about how someone had
seen me at the opera. And there were several people seri-

ously discussing if a gay porn star could really appreciate the opera. It was so funny.

"I didn't take part in the stupid conversation, but who cares if you are a porn star, or a ballet dancer, who cares? That's what you are. If you like opera, you like opera. It doesn't matter what you're doing. You don't have to transfer it anywhere. You don't have to transfer opera to your work; you don't have to be inspired by that.

"I guess there is inspiration everywhere. But I'm not going to take an opera scenario, opera movement, opera exaggeration, and opera drama, and create a gay porn movie based on that. I wouldn't do it, because that is incredibly cheesy and in incredibly bad taste, and I wouldn't do it."

But mixing opera and gay porn isn't the only thing Michael feels would be cheesy. A fan of fashion and a slave to designer labels, Michael Lucas knows fashion. "Talking about cheesy and about tacky," he continues, "I remember a party at *Interview* magazine I went to a week ago. There was a guy there whose book I could hardly read. His name is Andre Leon Talley, and he's the editor at large of *Vogue*.

"He was there talking about his book, *ALT* (his initials), and this man is incredibly powerful. The book isn't terrible, really. He's writing about his grandmother and about two women who inspired him in his life—his grandmother and Gloria Vanderbilt, who discovered him. When I read the book, I noticed a lot of fashion houses went on producing the long black gloves he described that both of these ladies like to wear. So everybody kissed his ass, producing right away for the coming season these long gloves.

"And I thought, 'Oh my God, that this person should be so incredibly powerful that everybody would have to suffer.' I saw him last week for the first time in my life, and he is so tacky I couldn't believe it—the way he acted, the way he moved, and what he was wearing. He was wearing a long coat—and he's like seven feet tall, maybe more—and he was wearing a huge piece of fur around his neck, really long. But I could not believe how tacky this man is.

"I was so confused because, as I was reading the book, I kept thinking how powerful he was and that he couldn't really be this tacky. Then after I saw him, I was thinking to myself how tacky he really is. He was bragging about beauty and elegance, and God forbid someone not clean the shoe, not make it shine perfectly—but also that the side shines, and every corner shines, and how tacky it is to wear this with that. He totally doesn't understand. He totally forgot about reality and lives in some strange century.

"He's eccentric, kind of like my friend Alexandre Vassiliev, but absolutely not. Andre Leon Talley was such a vulgar preacher. Sometimes it's just funny when you meet people in life before you see them, before you read about them, or before you read their book, and they are totally not what you expected. It's just interesting."

Michael feels so passionately about art—whether it's opera, fashion, photography, or exhibits in a museum—because of his family's background. He was brought up in a home where everyone was what is called "Russian intelligente," which in Russia was anyone who works with their brains and not their hands. If you are a teacher or an engineer, then you are Russian intelligente.

"Because of that, my grandmother was a teacher of music," recalls Michael. "And so my parents and grandparents were always taking me to the opera in Russia, and a lot of ballet." But photography also always interested Michael, which is possibly why he uses only the most skilled, most in-demand fashion photographers to shoot stills of his nude models. Michael recalls a rare find he scored when he lived in Europe.

"Two months before I came to America, the photographer Richard Avedon died. I had bought a photograph of

Rudolph Nureyev from a friend of mine, who actually died from AIDS. So his boyfriend sold it to me, and two months later, Richard Avedon died. I was always interested in theater, and I do collect some art, so Rudolph Nureyev was a very interesting character for me."

The photograph can be seen, and more from Michael can be read about Nureyev, on the August 12, 2005, entry on LucasBlog.com.

34

Michael reached another milestone in 2004 that increased his pride as a denizen of New York City, and of America. "In the United States, no matter what immigrant community you talk to, they feel very much at home," Michael says. "Immigrants are big-time patriots. They are loud patriots of the United States. From the first day, I felt at home. Because of the accent I have, it was always called 'cute,' even though I disagree. I'm going to school to try to lose the accent. But that's what Americans are saying, because they're very nice. But in Europe, try to speak to the French with an accent, they're going to put plugs in their ears and run away. So, you know, you'll never feel at home. But I feel at home here, which is why I'm going to be a good American."

In *The Soviet Jewish Americans*, Orleck also makes the point that the United States is not only good for immigrants, but also that immigrants are good for the United States. Michael Shapiro is an immigrant from Moscow who was concerned that the Immigration Reform act that was proposed in 1995 would keep his adult son from being able to come to the United States. Shapiro organized a letter-writing campaign to legislators in the Bay Area in opposition to the proposed act. Orleck quotes Shapiro from a speech he made to a diverse crowd of émigrés where he stated, "This country has been created by immigrants, and the diversity and the richness of their ideas and their talents have made this the greatest country in the world."

Just before the elections in 2004, Michael became a United States citizen. What happens in an election year is that the process of getting citizenship goes up to three times faster than it would without the potential voters. "I realized that when I came to do the fingerprints. I saw huge posters of Mr. Bush, so I figured he's trying to get more voters." Once someone lives in the United States for five years with his green card, he can apply for citizenship. On the paper he receives, he is told that it will take 560 days. But Michael applied in an election year. So, for him, the process only took five months.

Michael voted for Kerry and Edwards, and was just as devastated as everyone else when the results came in on "black Wednesday." Like other Americans, Michael was concerned that, since so much damage had been done in Bush's first term, what kind of horrors would befall the nation with another four years?

"The regime we have right now is totally antigay," Michael says. "Something to divide America, not to unite America. They're trying to divide gay people and straight people instead of bringing them together.

"It was a great opportunity we had after September 11, when the whole world was one, together with the United States. And this president, in four years, he did such damage. He not only alienated the whole world, he took respect away from the White House and the United States. He made America the most hateful nation in the world. And for me, as a gay man, I can't support a man who got to the White House for a second term by building hate between the gay community and the straight community, and separate them.

"I protested them during the Republican Convention in New York to show them that they are not welcome here— that here in New York, we party together. Gay people and straight people, we party together. That's very New York, and I hope will be America one day. All they're trying to do right now is bring up this divide between gays and straights so that people will forget about the economy, which the Republicans have no right to talk about because it's not good. And they can't talk about international politics, because it's shit, and this president created the worst diplomacy failure in history after 9/11. So all they're riding on is their 'family values,' by telling us that in creating our gay families, we'll destroy their straight families. This is the most disgusting thing about this cowboy."

By the time the holidays came around, many of us were still disheartened that Bush had won reelection. But you try to go on and just be grateful for the things you have— it's the spirit of the season. Michael and Richard felt the same way. Michael's business was doing better than ever; he was surrounded by good friends and his loving family, and he and Richard were throwing the Christmas party that, every year, now marks the anniversary of the time they met.

In their Manhattan apartment, 160 guests arrive to share in the joy of the season with New York's finest couple. The catering service is the same as last year and the year before that. Eight servers and two cooks make sure all the guests are satisfied and taken care of with the best food in town.

The guests always rave, after the party, that it was the best they've been to this holiday season, and that the food is amazing. The guests are an incredibly diverse group, with Richard bringing a very different crowd than Michael brings.

"And it's nice," Michael says. "There are older people and younger people. The majority of people are lawyers, doctors, politicians, and that's Richard's crowd. And a lot of my friends from the art world.

"We had Timothy Sanders [author of *XXX: 30 Porn Star Portraits*, which featured Michael] with his wife and daughter. Michael Musto, columnist for *The Village Voice*, was there. Hal Rubenstein from *InStyle* magazine was there with his boyfriend. And at some point in the evening, the furniture gets moved away to make room for all the people."

As Randy Jones, the cowboy from the Village People, was leaving the party, he overheard Musto say, "I can't believe all these people came to his party."

"A nasty comment, I thought," says Michael. "But then I thought, yes, all these people came to my party. He couldn't believe that all these people would come to a porn star's party. Yes, Mr. Musto, all these people came to my party, and you came to my party as well.

"And he enjoyed it very much. It is the greatest crowd, by far, great food and great liquor. So, of course, they came. Tons of celebrities, tons of New York celebrities—really, really intelligent people. Every year, it's the same. Every year, it's always very successful.

"Timothy Sanders brought lots of people, too. Mary Boone was there, the gallery owner. Timothy brought a lot of interesting people into my world. He was a big influence. When you're introduced by Timothy Sanders, it's a great introduction."

And finally, Michael brought in the New Year by bringing a bit of his childhood back into his world. "I hope one day to buy the country house, even though I will not really travel there," Michael says. "But it's killing me for some reason that this place doesn't belong to me anymore."

In the meantime, however, Michael called the current owners of the house and asked them if he could buy his great-grandfather's armchair. They readily agreed. Soon, the chair was being shipped from Russia, on its way to Michael in New York. "Stupid, right?" Michael says. "My parents could have just taken it, but they didn't ever think about it. I missed this armchair, and I wanted to buy it."

By the end of 2004, many sources of torment for Michael had come full circle, providing him with the closure he needed in order to move on with his life and his career. He collected on the bad check from Karim, his final payment from being an escort. He celebrated four years with his husband, a good man who came along at the perfect time in his life. Ivanna, his childhood love, got married and had a child. And he revamped the face of his company on the Internet in a way that has branded him at the top of his game.

Always the family man, Michael said he would absolutely marry Richard, but that he'll only do it in New York, and only if it's a legal marriage—either on a city, state, or national level. "And one day I hope to have a kid," Michael says. "So that would be very good, too." Judith Butler explains this dynamic in *Antigone's Claim: Kinship Between Life and Death*. She states, ". . . this is a time in which kinship has become fragile, porous, and expansive. It is also a time in which straight and gay families are sometimes blended, or in which gay families emerge in nuclear and non-nuclear forms." Richard isn't quite as keen on having children, but understands why Michael is thinking in that direction. "It's because he's always been so close to his family," Richard says. "And he'll want to continue that."

As Blake says, "Without Contraries is no progression." And Michael still has to deal with what his mother's illness will one day mean. However, Lena has accepted whatever will happen. Tired of the constant checkups, she has decided she no longer wants to know how far the cancer has progressed. She will just let it run whatever course it's going to take. Michael supports her completely, and is doing everything possible to make sure she's happy, comfortable, and can do as much as she can handle.

PART SIX

Master's Tea at Yale

As with any group whose history bears deep scars, expressing ourselves culturally—particularly through the gay-influenced worlds of fashion and the arts—is not a simple issue of leisure. It's a passionate matter of survival.

—Brendan Lemon

35

On April 20, 2005, Lucas Entertainment issued a statement notifying the press that Michael had been invited to speak at Yale University, and that he would present his speech there the following evening.

As part of the University's Master's Tea, the GaYalies group—one of six student organizations under the umbrella of groups dedicated to GLBT issues—had made Michael's appearance possible through their invitation. Michael's speech, set to take place at Calhoun College residential hall, was designed to include a question-and-answer session related to his work in the adult industry.

"The Master's Tea is one of those programs whereby someone notable who has done something of relevance and interest to the students is invited to campus to talk to students," said Yale Professor William H. Sledge, Master of Calhoun College, as quoted in the press release issued by Lucas. "Mr. Lucas came to our attention because of his responsible and clear positions on substance abuse and safe sex practices, a message that we feel is very important for youth of today."

In relation to Sledge's statement, the press release continued by touting an article that appeared in *The Advocate* several months earlier in which Harvey Fierstein discussed Michael's activism against porn with no condoms. Lucas had also taken out a full-page ad in an earlier issue of the same publication that spoke out against drug use in the gay community.

"I am honored to be invited to Yale to speak about these issues," Lucas said in the press release. "That a prestigious institution such as Yale recognizes them for discussion is a testament to how important and critical they are in this community right now."

Michael's speech was not open to the general public. Instead, only the faculty, staff, and students of Yale University were invited to attend.

36

MICHAEL'S SPEECH FOR THE MASTER'S TEA AT YALE

Thank you. I'm very honored to be here. My boyfriend, Richard, is from Yale University. It's actually my first time here. I'm very, very glad to be presented at Yale. I don't know what you're after. I think that we shouldn't concentrate entirely on safe sex issues, because it will be very boring. So whatever you guys want to ask me, please ask, and I will be glad to answer any question. You can ask me about my private life.

I'm from Soviet Russia, if you're interested in knowing anything about that. I always love to answer questions about that—about my years in Russia. I came here in 1997; I lived in Europe in 1995. Until '95, I lived in Russia. From '95 to '97, I lived in France, I lived in Germany. And then I came to the United States; I live in New York. So if you have any questions about Soviet Russia, I would answer you anything you want about it. Also I would answer anything you want about the adult industry—I know about both gay and straight, so please ask questions, and I would love to answer. I think it would be more interesting this way,

question/answer, right? Because I wouldn't know otherwise what you're interested in.

Should I sit down, do it sitting, or what is your practice?
Usually sit? Let's just sit. [audience laughter]

QUESTION: I know that you studied law in Russia, and I
wondered how is it that you made the transition from
being a law student to becoming a porn star and, ultimately, porn producer? And does your knowledge of law
help you in the business side of the porn industry?

MICHAEL LUCAS: Right. No, it did not. [audience laugh-
ter] But, you see, I had a great time in college. That's what
I wanted to do back then, and that's what my parents
wanted me to do. And it was a great time. In Russia, of the
schools you have to choose, you can go to university or
you go to work. So I could afford that. My family was a
middle-class family in Russia, very good family. My grandmother is a teacher of music; my grandfather was quite a
good engineer—famous engineer. My parents—well, my
mother was a teacher of Russian Literature. So I did that
because everybody in my family graduated. I did that; then
I left.

I wanted to leave Russia, and, you know, when you find
yourself in the West, I could not continue studying. I couldn't,
and I didn't really want to. So, it was easy for me to go into
the adult industry. And that's how I started. When I did start
my company, I was practicing international law. This has
nothing to do to help my company. So, no, it didn't help. It
didn't help at all. If it gave me anything for my life, it's just,
I think it's good to have an education in any field. It's good
for your brains, I guess, and for your knowledge. And I
have great friends, still, from university.

Q: I was just wondering if you could tell me a little bit
more about [incoherent], and what you see the future of
the gay porn industry [incoherent]?

ML: You have a loaded question. [audience laughter] All

right, it's about my new movie [*Dangerous Liaisons*]. Part of that, you know, I always was one who was saying that adult movies—I should watch my language—usually, in my opinion, the adult industry should work on producing movies that are there to help people to release themselves when they need to. It is not something about intellectual material. It's not about educational material. I always thought it should be as little plot as possible. [audience laughter]

But you know what? There were always all these directors—going from Chi Chi LaRue to John Rutherford from Falcon Studios [now with COLT Studio Group]—who always say, "The first thing I get is the idea of what is behind this movie—the idea." And I was always saying when they were asking "what is the idea behind the movie?" Well, it's sex behind it. Then they were asking me about the plot, and I said, "Well, the plot should be simple to connect the sex scenes." And I guess it did change my mind because—unfortunately or fortunately, I don't know, but—the truth is people want a story. I thought it's very pathetic, but who cares what I think about it? [audience laughter] They want the story, so I gave them the story.

I did like the movie, *Dangerous Liaisons*. I did like the book by Choderlos de Laclos, which I read back in Russia. It was interesting. It's very campy as well. Of course, that's what gay people like. [audience laughter] And I did this movie, and it was good, actually. Because I have a really great team. And I think my real talent is—because I'm not a film maker—my real talent, I think, is to surround myself with interesting people. I have thirteen people on staff in-house. Everybody is graduated from a good school. Everybody is a professional—except me—and I think that's my talent, to put these people together. And sometimes you have to challenge them and give them interesting projects; otherwise these people just burn out no matter how good

you pay. So it was great to see them working with such en-
thusiasm and being so interested in what they're doing.
And I think we've done a great, great movie together.

It was the first time we were choosing actors, not only
for their sexual abilities, but also for their ability to deliver
the dialogue. And the dialogues were great. I think I was
the worst one there, but everybody was just brilliant! We
had Gus Mattox who has a Broadway background and—I
guess he was not the most popular Broadway actor, but
[audience laughter]—he definitely shined in the movie. So
it turned out to be very, very interesting.

We got some B-list celebrities—C-list or A-list, I don't
know how we call them. We got Bruce Vilanch. We got
Harvey Fierstein. We got Timothy Sanders. We got Graham
Norton. We got all my drag queen friends, like Lady Bunny
and Hedda Lettuce. It was wonderful; we got Michael Musto
from *Village Voice,* Boy George, who is from the music
industry. They all made cameos, either through the film,
or they all made comments on the DVD behind the scenes.
So they did participate in different ways. Boy George did
write the music for my previous movie, *Manhattan Heat.*
So I think it's an interesting project.

It definitely gets more attention than any other adult
gay movie ever. That's great for me. We are receiving hundreds of pre-orders, and that's a great thing. That's a great
thing for my business. It has a beautiful style. I invited several fashion stylists. And I invited very talented, from makeup artists to camera people, to great photographers, stylists
on the set and stylists for the wardrobe. It was something
interesting, challenging, and something very, very different.
I liked doing this thing, actually, and I think it was worth it.
I think it will be a great project. People are waiting for it. It's
coming out the end of May.

Q: I was wondering, coming from Russia, like, looking
for opportunities in the West, how did you, kinda stumble

upon the adult film industry? Like, how did you make your breakthrough into that?

ML: Well, because I couldn't do anything else. [audience laughter] It's easy to drive a truck, which I didn't really want to. Or you continue studying, which I couldn't, and was not particularly interested in after five years of law school—that's how long it takes in Russia to become a lawyer, five years you study.

So I did start with fashion modeling. They said, "You have a very seductive . . ." seductive look? [audience laughter] It was a time when models had to be innocent-looking, and you know those guys who look very Eastern European boys. I was Eastern European, but since I'm Jewish—and that's not only religion in Russia; we had a paragraph that said nationality, it was not Russian it was Jewish, Russian, or Ukranian. It's very surprising to people in America, not surprising to people in Europe. But I don't look Slavic because I'm not. I guess I'm not because I don't think Jews ever assimilated in Russia. And so I have darker features and different features.

In Russia, I really don't fit into this Slavic, Eastern European look. But this look was popular, so I don't think I would make it. But I was never interested in—I was doing it for half a year and I got some unimportant covers, unimportant magazines, and unimportant shows. And it's all about staying in the lines for casting, and I hate going on castings, and I hate going on auditions. So I wasn't really interested in doing that. Then I started posing for nude photographers.

It started with me posing for guys who were in art school. And someone invited me to be photographed for this terrible magazine in Germany. That was my first nude work. Then I was invited by Cadinot—the biggest producer of adult movies in France, and he did two movies with me. And before that, I did one terrible straight movie in Germany—

and that was *really* disgusting. [audience laughter] No, no, not because it was straight—[audience laughter] but it was a *German* straight movie. So, you know. And so I was not thrilled. I maybe would be straight if not for that . . . [audience laughter] No, I'm kidding. Actually it was first straight movie; then there were gay movies. Then I worked for Falcon, I worked for Cadinot; then I opened my own company in 1998. Was that . . . ?

Q: You answered it.

ML: It was about my experience—why I didn't make it into something more grand? [audience laughter] Well, there was not a huge choice. But I'm very, very happy with what I did, because I don't think I would be able to meet people I was able to meet in any other industry. I would be a lawyer, or a truck driver, or whatever. I don't think my life would be that interesting. Because I have a very interesting life. I have very interesting friends. I have interesting opportunities, which are very often not presented. And there are a lot of people who—and me as well—who would love to be mainstream actors. But the opportunity is probably .0000001 percent.

So a lot of guys who would like to be in adult movies, or have a fantasy about it, or desire is they are waiting for the phone call from Hollywood. They make it very difficult on themselves, because they're also taking classes, and they're going to acting schools, and then they come to me for my auditions and they're about forty years old then. So I say, "Where have you been before?" And they say, "Well, I was waiting for this Hollywood call, and it never came." And I say "Well, I'm sorry. It's too late for you now." And then they go back to the bar. [audience laughter]

But I always was very realistic. You know, where can you get with this accent? And so I wanted to do something. And when I do something, I want it to be the best and the first. And I said I will be able to achieve it here in the adult industry. And I think I did achieve something here. My life is very interesting, so I'm very much satisfied. And I think you have more opportunities to do interesting things, and you have more opportunities to reach something, even in mainstream, if you are good at what you do in the industry I am in right now. So, for myself, I did a very right choice. At the same time, if you have any fantasies, keep them as fantasies. You're at a great school. You're the future of the country. You are great. And I think that's wonderful. Part of me is jealous of what you're doing. So let's go ahead.

Q: How do you feel about gay-for-pay in the adult film industry?

ML: I don't think about it. I prefer to work with gay guys, and in America I always work with gay guys. When I worked in Russia, they were all bisexuals or gay, but they're always saying that they are straight. You know, it's a very closeted culture. I went to Russia in the year 2000, and I did two movies there. But then when you go, I went to supervise a production in the Czech Republic. It was a new company, and I buy a lot of materials from Europe and from Eastern Europe—it's very cheap. So I went to supervise a production to kind of show them what American standard is and what the American market wants, and every guy was actually *really* straight. I mean, you actually had to give them Viagra or shoot them with an injection that's usually given to impotent people, and it goes directly to the penis. It's a liquid, and it drives your blood into your penis. And you're just hard automatically, where Viagra usually works with your brain, so for straight guys, it might not work very well. And they were really professional, and they were all straight, and they would do it to each other without any complaints, very professional, and faked it very well, and it was great. But that's the situation in Czech Republic, and they do everything. So that was totally fine with me. It's very different. Sometimes they're closeted, and I don't care what they think about themselves as long as they can do it.

As for myself, in America, I always work with gay guys. I would not have exclusive models, and I would never, ever get a straight guy and try to make him a star because their minds change much faster than—even gay guys very often, they go into the adult industry. You spend money on them and on building their image, and then they decide that they got into a relationship, or this or that, and they decide they don't want to do it—so with straight guys, they change their mind even faster. They find a girl, and the girl will say, "No, no. You can't do that."

In the Czech Republic, there were guys who came with their girlfriends. And the girlfriend would wait downstairs. If she came in, it would be hilarious. [audience laughter] They have this thing like a sexual revolution in Eastern Europe, and it's sometimes very campy and vulgar. But that's what's going on. Like in Russia, every woman is a hooker. Every gay guy is a hustler. Seriously, I was surprised. Well, not surprised—whenever they find out that you're from America, which in my case they treat me like I'm from America, they're very much interested in your money.

And when you go to, let's say, Brazil, it's very different, even when you are with a guy who is for pay; they don't make you feel like you're with a hustler. They make you feel very comfortable. Am I going into any area where we shouldn't go? [audience laughter] While in the Czech Republic, they would not let you have an illusion that you are not with a hustler. He's a hustler, and that means he's gonna complain about his difficult life. You know, old-style hookers, they're supposed to make you feel great and like you shouldn't think about—they shouldn't complain? Like there should be something about the illusion, they should also pretend that they're in love with you. Well,

that's what they do in Brazil. In Eastern Europe, they complain, complain, complain . . . [audience laughter] I mean,
everybody's dead in the family . . . [audience laughter] and
also they ask for everything . . . but I can tell you more
about those things, if you're interested. Go ahead.

Q: What do you think it is that kind of distinguishes you
from some lesser-known gay adult film stars? I mean, what
is it that makes an adult film star famous?

ML: What makes an adult film star famous? Well, I guess
you want to ask what makes an adult star stay in business
longer than other adult stars. What makes them become
famous for a year? That's Matthew Rush, if you know
who I mean. But very rarely do you stay in this business
for a long time. The first thing is that you have to have
your head on straight. You have to work, you have to look
great. And you have to change your look—not in a Madonna
way [audience laughter], because you are a man. [audience
laughter] You cannot dye your hair, you know? [To an audience member,] I'm sorry about that, by the way. [audi-
ence laughter] I did it, too, when I was 18. But no, I meant
Madonna. [audience laughter] Ohhh, God . . . anyway. [au-
dience laughter] I guess that, you have to change your
look.

When I started in the business, it was in '96 that I did
my first picture [chuckles], movie, film. I was very skinny.
I had long hair. And I was always changing. I became more
muscular, and I cut my hair shorter . . . I was always able
to look interesting, different, and good. And they were
saying, "Michael Lucas looks part of his age." And this is
possible when you don't party, when you don't drink, when
you don't do drugs. And this is very rare in this industry,
so that's why it's very easy for me to stay in this industry.
Because my background is great, and the background of
the competition is miserable. [audience laughter]

[a distraction occurs] ML: What's happening?

AUDIENCE MEMBER: It's a long story.

ML: All right, all right. Anyhow, I don't know if we should shut the windows or not.

AUDIENCE MEMBER: It will pass.

ML: It will pass? All right.

AUDIENCE MEMBER: Yes.

ML: Because why? You're not gonna give them what they want? [audience laughter] Anyway, so where are we? Oh yeah, about my looks, right. [audience laughter] If you look different from others, it's easy in this industry because in the background, it's quite a trashy background, it's easy to be different. And it's always about—I mean, my story is very different. I mean, every story of every porn star is, "Look at me, I was lying in the street with a needle in my vein. And look at me; this year I fuck in front of the camera like nothing ever happened." And that's great, you know, and "I was born in a trailer, and my mother abandoned me, and my father was beating me, and my grandmother was fucking me . . ." [audience laughter] And it's always—I didn't go through that.

I have a very different story. My childhood was flawless, and my teens were great, you know. My family is with me in America, and they know what I do. It's a liberal Jewish family, and they have no problem with it. My grandparents are 85 years old, and they moved here in the year 2000. Then my brother came, and my parents came. And my grandmother was asking me, "What you are doing tonight? Where are you flying?"

And I said, "I'm flying to Boston."

"What, are you performing there?"

"Yes, I'm performing in a club."

"Well, are they paying you?"

And to her, I would say, "Yes." Because she said, "That's good." Because such term as, I do it for promotions. In fact, I said if I came here, I would get a lot of money. Because she would not be happy. Because the terms of promotions would do something prestigious, just doesn't go well with her. She likes it when they give me cash. [audience laughter] Now, with my parents, they ask me what it is about, "Do they pay you?"

I say, "No, they don't pay me."

They say, "Oh, promotions."

They know. But my grandma is always about money.

But again, I was in the right place at the right time. And I have a great office staff and PR campaign that's fantastic. Well, I guess that's why I'm here. We're doing a very good job, and I always know what the journalists in my industry want. I always feed them new information, and I always find them something new to do. And that's why I'm still here for ten years, and it's going only up. What's the word? I think my status is improving because I think I'm one of the top porn stars, which is usually not the case when you're in the business for ten years—which is very nice. Let's go on.

Q: Looking generally at the adult entertainment industry, at your job, what is it you think you like most about your job?

ML: What do I like about my job?

Q: Yeah, I guess so, but just the industry at large. What do you think it provides that's positive?

ML: What, porn is good? [audience laughter] What? Make it simple for me—I'm a porn star! [audience laughter] No, I understand your concern. You want to know what is good about the adult industry. Well, I guess people sometimes want to save their time. The guys will understand me very well. I mean, we're offering you a beautiful, cute twink and whatever. You go to the bar, and you shine, but then again you go home alone. And then there is Michael Lucas to . . . [audience laughter] And Michael Lucas is there for you. [audience laughter] And that's very good, if you always have a condom. And you know what? Whenever you're tired of Michael Lucas, you shut him off and you don't have to—it's disappointing to go home with someone. You have to take this person home. You have to watch your wallet. Then when it's all over, you keep thinking, "Won't he leave?" [audience laughter] "Please, don't fall asleep." Because they sometimes get too comfortable, and they want to sleep with you. And you really don't feel like it, you know. Anyway. It's a lot of work to have a trick, especially if you have to get up at 8:00 in the morning. That's where porn is great. Now also, we can go there that, it's very often it is educationally very well in terms of safe sex.

Unfortunately, only Vivid is the straight company that uses condoms. Most of the gay companies are for safe sex, and we use condoms. My company always uses condoms. And that's very good for our—And it's very good also for people who are not educated on sex issues, somewhere in Nebraska. I don't think it's really widely available. So they see that you can have sex, and have fun, and have a great time, and still use condoms and be safe. And that's great. Because today, especially in New York, people think that you cannot have a good sex life without using drugs.

And it's incredibly sad because, you know, I never actually tried drugs. And I don't recommend anyone trying them ever. For me, my model worked perfectly well. I never tried them, so I never was intimidated. And I think it's incredibly sad when people lose their ability to have fun because they learned it's maybe more fun to have it on drugs. It's obviously good, I believe. Otherwise, why would they spend their money and be in this terrible suicidal mood the next day? I mean, there are so many bad things about it. So, I'm sure the high is great. But I decided for myself that I wouldn't do it. I just would never try it, and I'm so happy about that. It also makes me a little pe-

culiar—not only in the adult world, in the porn world—
but also in New York City, and I like it.

I don't drink. I don't smoke. And I enjoy it because it
makes me different. I like to be different. And I think it
also gives me a chance to stay in my business, in front of
the camera, longer. And I do really recommend you all not
to try it, and if you tried it, just forget it. It makes your life
so much better. Drugs are incredibly dangerous, and I
think that we all should be very much in control, especially
when it comes to sex.

You know, when I moved to the West, in order to make
money to start my production company, I had to be a hustler. And I was hustling for three years. And it was fine. It
was a difficult job. I enjoyed it in my own way. I was good
at it. But you know what? I never, ever had any sexual contact with a disease—I mean nothing. And I think it's because I always used my head—common sense—and that's
because I never used drugs, alcohol. I was always sober
and in control, and when you have sex four or five times a
day, you should be in control. And since we are talking
about that, I do really advise you all, when you have sex,
no matter how good it is—and sometimes, and I'm sure
you've all been in this situation—in the moment you forget about, and you don't want to think about condom use.
Because we all know it feels better to have sex without a
condom. I mean, it's true. But it's so not worth it. Not only
is it not worth it because you can get sick, but it's also not
worth it because of how you feel in the next moment when
it's over. You always feel guilty. You always have . . . you're
scared. And you always know that it was wrong. And I
don't think that this moment—this minute, or sometimes
hours [audience laughter]—I don't want this excitedness
that we all know about.

Everyone, I'm sure, once or twice, made a mistake. And
I'm sure everybody will make this mistake once or twice,

feel bad about it, feel guilty about it, so it's not worth it. And if you use a condom, you just feel good about yourself. You feel good about yourself, and that's what is important. It's a difficult time we're living in, and we have to play by these rules. It's always worth using a condom, even if you're not on drugs; always use a condom. AIDS is a very difficult virus to get—very difficult virus to catch—but surprisingly, lots of friends of mine got it in the past year. I mean, many actors and many friends, they got it last year. And lots of them were not drug users. Many of them got it from their lovers, who cheated on them, and that's another problem. A lot of people get it, and they are quite innocent. They get it from people they trust.

So very often, you should think about whom you're dating. Sometimes, you can be with a person for years, and you don't really know him. Because people lie a lot. Or people don't want to know because they're scared. Lots of people are scared to be tested. So when they're telling you they're not positive, they're scared. Sometimes it's just the right thing to do is to keep having your relationship and using the condom. Very often, it's worth it, you know? But then it's your choice. Again, how far do you want to trust your friend, your boyfriend? Because in the end, it's about your life, and that's more important than to ruin the moment and say, "Come on. We have to go get tested together. Then we'll decide if we want to have a relationship without using condoms and having intercourse without condoms." Because everything else, I would believe is safe, or 95 percent safe. But having intercourse without a condom is, of course, a dangerous thing. And you have to think twice before doing that with your loved ones. That's what I believe. In the end, it's all about you. He's gonna be gone one day—well, hopefully not—maybe he will be gone, and then it's all about you. So it's just worth thinking about that.

Q: I know that you're in a relationship, and . . . I was wondering how you handle . . . ?

ML: Well, it happens that I was always in a relationship. I'm now in a relationship for five years. See, in different relationships, it's worked differently. My boyfriends would have to be open-minded men. The boyfriend I have right now, he is the president of the Gay & Lesbian Community Center in New York City. He graduated here, from Yale. And he was working for a Boston consulting group. Now he's doing charity work for Gay Community Center, and Bisexual and Transgender Center—and everything in between. And he's a very open-minded man. He's also 49 years old; I'm 34. I mean, he's a great-looking man, beautiful man, inside and outside.

Again, stressing it's very different from my previous relationship that was for four years with an American from Georgia, from a very religious family, where they had five kids. But he was very much damaged, I believe, by his family. And he had a problem with me doing what I'm doing. And he was trying to suppress me, and he was getting on my nerves. It's always very bad in a relationship to press on your partner, and trying to prevent him from doing something he believes is good. Either leave him, or let him do what he's doing. So we had all these fights, and, in the end, I had to break up with him. And I understood after that, that I cannot date . . . [audience laughter] from Georgia. Because it just wouldn't work. If I would be in a different business I was good at, I would love it. But he has a problem with that, because of his family, his background. His father would have a heart attack if he would know what I'm doing. We'd always have to come up with lies. Thank God, my boyfriend now, his family is all dead. [audience laughter] I don't have to lie.

With my family, I don't have to lie. They are very comfortable, and we can talk. They would probably choose

me to be a lawyer, but I'm a pornographer, and they're not running hysterical about that. They're just asking me not to tell their other relatives, not to make them happy about that. So, when it comes to a relationship, I always want a relationship. It's very easy to be in a relationship, especially if you live in New York City. To find a boyfriend, or a girlfriend, is really easy. It's a very easy thing to do because there are so many people. You have a great choice. So when someone lives in New York City, when he complains, "Oh my God, I can't find a relationship. Why can't I get in a relationship?" He's full of shit. [audience laughter] There's something terribly wrong with this person. [audience laughter] This must be so, because everybody's looking. I mean, I was never really looking for a relationship. I was always perfectly fine to be by myself for several months. It just always happened so that someone . . .
[TAPE BREAK]

You never can have a normal conversation or anything with them. They always complain how bad the world is, that all men are pigs. And no one wants a serious relationship, and you can't find a guy, not on the Internet, not in a nightclub. It's just a nightmare. If that's all they can talk about, and that's their life, it's a constant struggle to get a man. They wake up in the morning, and they think . . . Lately, there's a tendency in the gay world for gay men to look like straight men—to have a family, to have a boyfriend, to have a husband, to have a wife, to have children. You know? They will all go now and buy these Filipino babies on the Internet. [audience laughter] It's true. I think it is nice that we are different, you know? And if someone wants to have a baby, it's beautiful. But now there is an obsession with babies. Everyone has to have it.

I was filming a picture, and the people who lived across the hall—they're actually my neighbors, he was actually my dentist, and I pay a lot of money to my dentist—yes, this beauty is not natural. He called the police on me, so I called him, and I said, "It's me, Michael Lucas."

And he said, "Oh, it's you! You're terrible. You're filming porn on my floor!"

I said, "Of course, I have to pay your bills." [audience laughter]

And he said, "My kids..." He bought Puerto Rican kids. [audience laughter] And he thinks he's much better than any gay man who doesn't have kids.

And I said, "Listen, there's no harm in my shoot. The whole hallway away from you is much farther away than your bedroom, where as far as I know, there's a sling." [audience laughter] Then he complained again to the board. He's a member of the board of this beautiful building. He wrote me a letter, that I should still be his client. It's unprofessional; it's nothing to do with business.

And he said, "This is a family building." As a gay man, he said, "This is a family building. How dare you? How dare you do that in a family building?"

And that coming from a gay man is disgusting. Straight people are less conservative, very often, than those gay people who bought babies. [audience laughter] And he thinks that he is gay upper-class, and he lives in a family building, which makes me very upset. Because, you know, I think it's good that gay people are different, and we should be different. Let's go to next question. Okay, we'll go here, and then we'll go to you.

Q: How much of a problem in the U.S. and/or Europe would you say child exploitation is?

ML: I don't know anything about exploitation in terms of the adult industry.

Q: Well, you know, just underage—

ML: I saw that in Russia, when I went in the year 2000. I called several escort agents because that's what they have tons of right now. And they start to send me these 16-year-old kids, 15 and 16, and that's so scary. I requested ID, you know, before they entered the door. Because I called them, I said, "You cannot do it."

And they were very surprised. They said, "They're adults. They're 15, 16; they know what they want."

And I was talking to one kid; I said, "How old are you?" He said, "I'm 15."

He looked like he was 20, or whatever, and I said, "What's this all about?" And he told me this sad story. He told me that he has to make money to study. I told him goodbye, and after that I requested ID before they came to the casting. In America, they would never enter my office without showing me ID. But they never come in America—the youngest would be 18. But usually my models are over 20, 25, 30, 35, 40. But in Europe that happens. But in America, you cannot distribute porn, and you will get in such hell of a trouble—and thank God, you will—if you work with kids. And we have to request two pieces of picture IDs. If you don't have two picture IDs—very clear, government-issued picture IDs—there will be no conversation. I mean, you will be out, no matter how old you look. I guess in Eastern Europe, there's . . . and I'm sure it's a big problem in Asia as well.

It's a big problem in Thailand. Thailand is the bordello of the world. And they say, "It's our tradition." I was talking to a lot of guys from Thailand, and they said, "You guys, Westerners, don't know what the hell you're talking about. It's our tradition, you're trying to destroy it." They would tell me, "When I was 12, my brother took me to the bordello, and there was a girl who was 14, and we had a great time. And I would have had a better time, but I was gay, but I still had a good time." [audience laughter] But that is a terrible, terrible thing. I mean, tradition or not. I think this tradition should be destroyed. That's my opinion, because when you're 12 years old, you have to have a normal childhood—like I had, and look what happened. [audience laughter]

Anyway, that's what I feel very strongly about, that I would never work with anybody who is under 18 years old. I think it's wrong. It's terrible, and thank God it's—I think—under control in the United States. And it's under control in Western Europe. I think in Eastern Europe they do it. But they can't distribute it into the West. They can't distribute it because, for one to take such terrible risks, you can't sell it in the stores. I guess it's for sale on the Internet. But they catch those people who are watching it. So, yes.

Q: I wanted to, first of all, add to something you said earlier. My boyfriend left for Romania yesterday. So, last night, Michael Lucas, you were there for me. [audience laughter]

ML: I'm very thankful! [audience laughter]

Q: But we watch your work, and the work of others, together. For couples, pornography can add an interesting dimension to their love-making. But, on a different topic . . .

ML: Could you send it over? [audience laughter]

Q: Sure. Another topic is the issue of barebacking. I graduated from Yale in 1995. At that time, the porn industry had done a very good job of policing itself in suppressing bareback films. Now, if you were to go on a major Web site, like RAD Video, one of the first things you see are bareback videos right at the top of the page. What is driving the new demand for bareback porn? Is it . . .

ML: The demand.

Q: Do you think people's sexual practices are as careless as what they want to watch on TV?

ML: No, it's different. Sometimes, it's careless. Sometimes they are very safe in their life, but they still want to watch these porn videos. The thing is, there's a lot of money there, because a lot of people like bareback sex because it's hot. But what is not hot is the guys. In my opinion, you wouldn't get these guys to do bareback films. You would get [audience laughter], you would get a very freaky-looking guy. Very freaky-looking guys to do bareback films. The guys, good-looking men, no matter if he's HIV positive or not, he will not go and do the terrible barebacking films. And you see, there's a big difference, you know? Anyway, these guys are usually very freaky-looking. [audience laughter] And they're usually on drugs—not because of their status, I don't know their status; I don't want to know their status—they look bad. They're on drugs.

I saw a couple of these films. They are on drugs; they're sick-looking. They don't care for themselves. No one in his own mind will go and do bareback films. It destroys your reputation. And you're basically sending the message that, "I don't care, and I'm very sick, and I want to live a very short life." Nobody in their own mind will do it. And when you see, I mean, you will never get good-looking guys to do it. They're not competition to us, they're not competition to Falcon, they're not competition to Kristen Bjorn. It's very sad that it's there. And this is the issue where I think the government should step in and should put an end to that. And I think it's gonna happen. They should do it, because it's very bad for people to see it. It might confuse people and send the wrong message.

When you ask what is different between, why it's so easy for me to stay in the industry, because when they ask me for the cover, I give them the cover. When *Hot House* asks for the cover, they give it the cover. I think it's very easy for me because I use great people, great—you know, I do very different stuff. And it's very easy to give them a class-act in porn. Again, it's all about competition. There is none. So it's easy. [audience laughter] Next.

Q: Which porn star have you enjoyed working with the most?

ML: What porn star I enjoyed working with the most? Didn't care, really. [audience laughter] I can't really, there is no one in my mind that I can tell you, Joe Blow was so good; I just can't forget him. No, really, I never had relationships with porn stars. Porn stars are usually very needy. They're very needy people, very complicated people. They're hysterical, and hilarious. And some exclusive actors, you know, you have to be very close with them because they're your exclusives. And they always tell you these tragedies about their lives. I mean, I have one guy, Wilfried Knight. He is my exclusive for one year, and I think I have about 118 hours from him. And every e-mail is that his life is terrible, or he's asking for something. And so, I never had the idea to be in a relationship with a porn star.

And I never was really friends with a porn star, because usually they are complicated people. That's why they go into this business. People in show biz are very complicated. They're not your ordinary people, and especially in the adult industry. So it's a little bit not my world, just because it's too much work. I did help many of them. And I realized it's really not a good idea to help them. A good example is—I don't know if you know him—Kent Larson. He's a big model today. He called me and said, "I'm broke. I'm out of the house, and I don't know where I'm gonna live any longer. I don't have a place. Can you guarantee my apartment?" And I was very stupid, and very irresponsible, to guarantee his apartment. He was there for three months. Then he called me and said, "It was very irresponsible of me to ask you for the apartment, because now I cannot pay it." So in the end, I had to pay for one year, basically for his apartment. Sometimes, he would perform for me for free. So basically, you want to help. But by giving them that help, you're basically destroying them because they cannot put their act together. Then in the end, you don't have a good relationship with this porn star because you can't keep yourself from e-mailing him back and saying, "Listen. You are a 31-year-old man, six-foot-four tall, and 250 pounds. And you're American, and I came to this country. I had nothing. I worked hard, and I didn't speak English very well. I learned English, I worked hard, I opened my company. I brought my whole family here. I am great, and you are a piece of shit. [audience laughter] You were born here, and you are this great-looking guy. Why don't you hit the road, and make money, and pay this bloody $1,000 for your apartment in Dallas?" Then he goes around, and he bad-mouths you, just because he's not able to go back in his head and think, "Okay, he guaranteed my apartment, and I cannot pay for it. He's a little bit pissed." No. He will tell that Michael Lucas is terrible. So, if I hadn't helped him, it would still be great. He would still work for me. He will go out and tell what a great experience it is to work for Michael Lucas.

MODERATOR: So we're almost out of time. So maybe one more?

ML: Do we have anybody new? Those two guys.

MODERATOR: Okay.

ML: I will make it short. I will stay on the subject. [audience laughter] Go ahead.

Q: What are your thoughts on civil unions?

ML: If I have a thought on civil unions? It's a great thing. It's very moving, civil unions. I would think gay marriage is the important thing. I think since we are paying taxes, you know we've all talked many times, and I have the exact same opinion, I guess, as the majority of gay people. I think we are paying taxes, and we should have the same rights. And civil union is a . . . and it's nice if they will pass gay marriage. Because it exists already in Europe. The institution itself was dying in Europe, so they didn't care if they gave it, in some countries, to gay people. And if they want people to keep this institution alive, why not give it to gay people? Gay people still want it; nobody else does. [audience laughter] America is so oppositional. Of course, we have to have all the rights that straight people do.

Q: You said something very interesting. You said it would be great if maybe the government had a revelation about the foolishness and popularity of unsafe videos. But I think maybe you're opening a Pandora's box. Aren't you maybe a little more concerned, if you thought about it, that this government—the government of the United States— if Christian conservatives got their hands on the regulation of pornography in America, that they would put you out of business? My question is, do you ever feel any kind of danger from the political conservatives?

ML: Yes. But I think they're so busy with Iraq right now that they wouldn't have time for us, for a new battle. But you know on the other hand? They found time for this vegetable girl, what her name was? [audience laughter] This president—there were thousands of men and women dying in Iraq every day, in Africa, in Asia—and this idiot drives Air Force One with taxpayer's money, to save the life of this vegetable and have a speech about her. You know what? I was always thinking, if she's that smart— you know because she can smile, she can burp, and she can piss [audience laughter]—how about one burp for yes, two burps for no?

But it's a huge industry. I think if they go after anyone, they will go after straight companies first, like Vivid. We don't really make much difference, you know, gay companies. But at the same time, demand is so huge. Really, it's a billion-dollar business. I don't know if they will go after porn. But who knows? They do ridiculous things. You never know.

And I'm glad that I amused you a little bit. [audience laughter and applause] Thank you very much, and I have some business cards I can pass around. If you have any additional questions, join my Web site. It's for free—if you are an intellectual. If you want . . . it's for money. [audience laughter] But I will pass you my business card. And thank you very much for coming over. I'm very, very, very touched that you all came. And you are the future of the country, and we're proud to be here. So thank you very much.

37

YALE DAILY NEWS
Published Friday, April 22, 2005
Adult film producer fleshes out his 'fantasy' at tea
by Kevin Osowski, Staff Reporter

One seldom has the opportunity to attend a Master's Tea with a porn star. Calhoun College, in a partnership with gaYalies, fulfilled the dreams of about fifty sexually charged students on Thursday by hosting Michael Lucas, a gay porn producer and star of numerous adult films.

Lucas spoke with students about sexual politics, the porn industry and his experiences as a Russian immigrant. After studying international law in Russia, Lucas lived in France for two years before moving to the United States. After beginning his career as a nude model, Lucas began acting in pornography.

Lucas started his adult film career with a short stint in heterosexual porn, but said the experience was unfulfilling.

"It was really depressing . . . not because it was a straight movie, but because it was a German straight movie," he said through a thick Russian accent.

Lucas then worked as a hustler—earning money through

prostitution to open up his own porn production company in New York City. Today Lucas heads Lucas Entertainment, a company that produces and distributes adult gay films featuring men representing the diverse ethnic makeup of New York.

Lucas said he believes in the work he does because porn "helps people relieve themselves." Though Lucas admits that his work is not "intellectual material," he does attempt to aim higher than simply selling sex scenes. His latest project is an all-gay adaptation of the film "Dangerous Liaisons." It has been billed as the "biggest gay adult production ever," and he said it features cameos by famous gay celebrities. Lucas said his new film is "very campy . . . of course, that's what gay people like."

Lucas stressed safe sex and condemned drug use several times during the tea. He said that he owes his health and career to the fact that he never tried drugs.

"In the end, it's about your life, and that's most important," Lucas said.

When asked for his key to success, Lucas paused for reflection.

"My talent is to surround myself with interesting and talented people and to give them a challenging project to work on," he said.

On the subject of politics, Lucas' views were simple.

"Gay marriage is a great thing . . . we're paying taxes and we should have the same rights," he said.

But even though he said he believes gays should have the right to marry, Lucas said he does not think they should.

"There's a trend now in the gay world to look like straight men—to have a husband and a wife and a baby. They're ordering these children from the Philippines," Lucas said disdainfully, adding that he thinks gay men should be happy being different.

Lucas's view on government intervention in the porn industry surprised many in the audience. Though he said he believes the government should put an end to films that encourage unsafe sex, he does not believe the Bush administration will crack down on pornography.

"They're so hung up with the Iraq thing now that they wouldn't have time for it," Lucas said.

Lucas was received relatively well by the students who attended yesterday's tea.

"He provided a refreshing perspective from someone you wouldn't usually see here," Tre Borden '06 said. "I thought a lot of his opinions were well informed."

A visiting pre-frosh, Daniel Waldinger, and his family also attended the event and said they found it both entertaining and informative.

"I just didn't know that people were advocating for reforms in the industry," Waldinger's mother, Jennifer Stone, said.

Though he's happy with his career and claims to have a "very interesting life," Lucas provided some simple advice for Yalies with dreams of entering the porn industry.

"If you have a fantasy, keep it as a fantasy," Lucas said.

38

It is incredibly interesting, after reading the transcript of Michael's address at Yale's Master's Tea, to read the article about Michael's appearance that was published by the *Yale Daily News*. Michael hadn't talked about people adopting Filipinos disdainfully. It was very lighthearted, and the audience roared with laughter. He wasn't received *relatively* well; they *loved* him. He was received *very* well. Some of the quotes in the article weren't exactly how he had stated them, but still kept their intended meaning. The article also said there were 50 people there, when there were actually about 120.

This is one minor example of how coverage of even an event this public can be presented in a way that could be detrimental to the subject. Michael deals with these kinds of misunderstandings daily on his blog (www.LucasBlog.com). Readers post comments to his entries often disagreeing with points he has made, and those are his own words! But Michael's appearance at Yale was not diminished in any way by the article.

Yes, Michael Lucas had joined company with other greats who had spoken at the Master's Tea at Yale University— people like John McCain, Oliver Stone, Meryl Streep, Kurt

Vonnegut, and Larry Flynt. "My trip was very good," Michael says of his prestigious appearance. "I've never been to Yale, and my boyfriend graduated from there. All his friends graduated from Yale. It was very interesting for me to see what it is like, and I felt it when they sent a limo to pick me up.

"It's a beautiful drive, really. I had forgotten how beautiful it is outside of New York, you know, the nature. But it was New Haven, Connecticut. The area is beautiful. But when we were driving in, it felt like the horrible movie *Legally Blonde*. I felt like that."

Michael, gushing at the beauty of the town and the university, said to his assistant, who had accompanied him, "Oh, it's really cute! I like it here!" Michael says that the town and the university were so clean and spectacular, and he was impressed by the boutiques, restaurants, and cafés that lined the streets.

They met Michael and his assistant there and introduced them to Professor William H. Sledge, Master of Calhoun College.

"How many people do you expect to attend?" Michael asked him.

"Ten or twenty," answered Master Sledge. "We'll see. It's a beautiful day."

However, when 120 people showed up to hear Michael speak, the professor was shocked and impressed. "My God," he said. "The power of sex!"

Michael gave his address in a beautiful, wooden room with eighteenth-century paintings in gold frames. He found the style very comfortable and delivered his question/answer-formatted speech in nearly an hour and a half. "I was very happy," Michael says. "I was very proud. I did understand right away that it's an honor to go to Yale. And as a porn star, as a porn entrepreneur, you're not always accepted. But if Yale accepts you, and invites you, and pays for your transportation, invites you for dinner and treats you well, and puts you in Yale's newspaper, I think that others should look at that and endorse me as well.

"It's good for the whole adult industry. This is acceptance. But they made a good choice, I think. At least I didn't embarrass our industry. They asked if everybody was like me, and I said, 'Oh, no. They're *not!*'"

PART SEVEN

Michael Lucas—Czar of Gay Porn

It is better to be hated for what one is than to be loved for what one is not.

—André Gide

39

By saving money, reinvesting, and using all the financial and personal resources at his disposal, Michael has built his company up from nothing. Before, when companies didn't want to help him succeed—like with the duplication of VHS copies—he had no choice but to accept the price he was given. Today, if he were to call a company for such a service, things would be different. However, Michael doesn't make those calls anymore.

"I have ten companies a month calling me with their proposals," Michael says. "And it always starts with 'We love your company. We're dying to work with you. We will beat the price of any competitor.' Well, it was not like that in 1998. I had to make calls, and they would never return them. It's all about building your name, building the respect, and after that, everything just comes to you. You don't have to run after anybody; they're lucky to get the money.

"It's a lot of hard work. In 1998, I was working by myself. It was only the beginning of '99 when I got an assistant, and a long way until the day when I ended up with three departments here—production department, computer department, and public relations department. Plus, we have bookkeepers, accounting, and all the freelancers who are working for me.

"And then now we have the distribution department, which is a fourth one. And now I'm hiring the person who is going to be filming and editing in-house, and this is something new. In terms of my career, I have millions of plans. We're distributing our films ourselves, and we have a five-person distribution department. And we've also started distributing the products of other companies like Lucas Kazan, Marcos Studios from Brazil, and Titan in New York."

Lucas Distribution also recently signed three companies from Europe in its efforts to create a significant distribution department. Lucas Entertainment has three lines of its own—the most important one is Manhattan Productions in New York, Fire Island Productions, and Lucas International. Michael has started hiring new directors to direct films for the company in Europe, but he remains, as always, famous for New York.

T. Hitman, a writer for *Unzipped* magazine, says that Michael puts an interesting, visible, and respectable face on gay pornography. "He's a genius," says Hitman. "He's really set the bar higher. He's a star, let's face it. I review a lot of movies for the magazine. Something I like about Michael—which is one of the things I kind of like about Chi Chi LaRue as well—is that his pornography is fresh and exciting and different, not tired and formulaic. What I like about Michael Lucas is his vision. He's not afraid to trot out the unexpected."

Hitman says it's fair to say that Michael doesn't even really set the bar for the porn industry, because his productions are so far above it, particularly with his film *Dangerous Liaisons*. Comparing Michael's work to that of rival gay porn director Chi Chi LaRue might have some legitimacy, but the way they do business is vastly different. It has been the source of a professional ulcer between the two of them, who were once friends and business partners.

The way Michael runs his business has been strong and sometimes brutal. Friends of Michael say that they sometimes wish he would be more careful at choosing his battles, that not everything demands such swift justice when he doesn't get his way. But it all goes back to Michael's knowing what he wants—and getting it. It's the reason he's been so successful. However, his friends worry that he may alienate people in the industry who might be able to help him in the future.

However, Michael does have his standards and will not let anything stand in the way of them. Michael, true to his standard and well-known policy on drugs, fired model Rob Ramos over a drug addiction. Chi Chi, who was responsible for providing a trophy boy for the GayVN awards on Michael's birthday in March, hired Ramos for the task. "There are only two trophy boys," says Michael. "And I was supposed to go there and stand on the stage with Rob Ramos.

"I was surprised, because Chi Chi knew the story, and knew that I had fired him for drugs. And I am the distributor for her company in New York—well, I *was*."

"Chi Chi, I'm not sure I understand," Michael said on the telephone. "Why do you have Rob Ramos as a trophy boy? We agreed that I have a problem with him."

"Michael, you have to get over that," said Chi Chi. "He looks very good. He was very nice to me."

"It's really irrelevant whether he was nice to you or not. You mean that he was doing drugs because I am a bitch? He caused me problems. He cost me a whole production day. And I'm not interested in staring at him and seeing him be rewarded by you, whom I consider my friend."

"Michael, you have a lot of people in your movie *Dan-*

gerous Liaisons whom I hate. So what would you do if I called and said you shouldn't deal with them?"

"It's no question. Right away, this person would be out of the picture."

"Well, but I would never use my power like that."

"That's an irrelevant comment again, Chi Chi. I'm sorry, but it seems to me like you are stupid. You're all the time using the arguments that are irrelevant. You ask me what I would do, and I'm answering to you. If you called me—you asked me what I would do—I said I would fire this person without question. You know why? Because actors are actors; they come and go. And that's not even an exclusive actor, and he is a drug addict. Of course, I will choose to take your side."

"Well, I will never use my power this way."

"Well, that's again irrelevant." After the conversation kept going in circles this way for a few more minutes, Michael finally said, "I hope you wouldn't do it. I can't stop you. You are a very important person to deal with."

Ultimately, for whatever reasons, Chi Chi made the decision to keep Ramos as a trophy boy for the award presentation. When Michael went on stage to accept his award, he would not take it out of Ramos's hand. So Ramos put the award on the podium.

Michael, who will be the first to tell anyone that he does not take himself or porn too seriously, gave his acceptance speech for the award by saying, "It's very nice. Thank you for giving me this award. And it's my birthday, so it's a good gift. I'm thirty-three years old now; it's like Jesus's age. And I'm very similar to Jesus. First, we are two Jewish boys. And second, there are so many of you right here in this audience who would like to crucify me."

While many in the audience found the comment funny, many people in the industry took the comment too seriously and criticized him harshly. The first thing Michael did when he returned to New York was have his office assistant send all of Chi Chi's product back to her. He cut her from his distribution. Michael's short e-mail to her manager said, "Mr. Rob, I didn't tell you to talk to Chi Chi, and you told me that it's none of your business. And you said, 'Michael, I'm only the business manager; I don't interfere in that. Let's not put together business and entertainment.' I said, 'You are in show business. Show business is a combination of show and business. So if you let Chi Chi run the show, and you are going to take care of business, then your business is going to suffer because she is not playing a fair game. So that was my point. You missed it. Now take your movies and shove them up your ass.'"

Michael's choice was to disregard the income his distribution company would have made from Chi Chi's business in order to stand up for his feelings about drug use in the industry. "Why this business is so fucked up is because of people like Chi Chi LaRue making wrong choices," Michael says. "To choose between a model who is on drugs or the president of a distribution company should be a no-brainer. She's making the choice to work the model. That's sick. But that's where I am."

Chi Chi, who as recently as last year spent Thanksgiving with Michael and his family, refused to comment about the incident with Rob Ramos and the GayVN awards. Chi Chi's and Michael's competitive natures have created a lot of buzz within the gay porn industry since the incident. And it's that same competitive nature that sent Chi Chi into a jealous tirade when she discovered that Michael, like Jenna Jameson, was coming out with a book. "He is very good at self-promoting himself," she sneered. "And he is nowhere near as famous as Jenna Jameson." But many in the industry disagree with her.

What Chi Chi doesn't understand—which even Michael, in his similarly competitive nature, understands very well—

is that the two of them really aren't in competition at all. They both produce very different products, and there is a demand for both of theirs, as well as the many other companies producing high-quality gay porn today.

Even John Rutherford, whose experience with Michael at Falcon could have ended in similar verbal fisticuffs as a result of Holmes's disinterest in promoting Michael, says there is room on the shelf for everyone. "Michael's always playing with danger," says Rutherford. "That's his thing; he likes it. I think his responsibility as a businessman is to treat others in the industry with respect, and he's always treated me respectfully. He's never done anything to me. People can talk badly all they want. And if they're jealous, that shows their weakness. COLT Studio Group has a strong brand, and we're kicking ass. I don't want to think about what everybody else is doing. I never have."

Rutherford makes an excellent point. The measure of success is not in comparing your work to others. It is about doing better than the last one you did, building yourself up. You can only measure your success against yourself. That's what people know who are in the number-one spot.

40

After his appearance in Timothy Greenfield-Sanders's book *XXX: 30 Porn Star Portraits* (and its accompanying HBO special), and Lucas Entertainment's most successful year yet, Michael continues to bitch-slap stereotypes and stomp the stigmas of the gay porn industry and explode into the mainstream. He does so without apology or pretense, and simultaneously raises the bar of expectation for the entire gay porn industry. He is making it all happen with the production and highly anticipated release of his current project, *Dangerous Liaisons* (www.Dangerous LiaisonsXXX.com).

The Web site for the film has a blog that discussed elements of the production in real-time as it was being made. This behind-the-scenes strategy, which began with a casting call, has created an interest for the film that is just one of the film's gay porn firsts. "We started advertising this production months before we started shooting, saying 'this is what we're going to do,'" says Michael. "It started with 'we are now casting,' then 'now we are preparing,' 'now we are photographing.' It was a whole different production and a different campaign."

What makes this film different from every other porn

production may have begun with behind-the-scenes interest, but has continued into the very core of its production. Michael and his cast and crew worked from seven in the morning until about ten at night every day. They worked through weekends and steered the production toward a final wrap party that doubled as a nonsexual shoot for the film. It was a lot of work, but Michael says that his team was fully prepared to reach the goals of the project.

Lucas Entertainment is a well-known company, but Michael wanted to bring it up to a different level with the creation of this film. He wanted to create a showcase. Michael says that when people asked him what his favorite production was, he didn't know what to say, because they're all good. With *Dangerous Liaisons*, he wanted to have something that was different from everything else he had done so far, and from what everyone else was doing.

Michael got the idea for the film after reading *Les Liaisons Dangereuses* by Choderlos de Laclos, and based the idea for his film on the book. Next, he researched other films based on the novel. Talk and print related to Michael's project soon began, comparing it to the Hollywood version with Glenn Close and John Malkovich (1988). "If you check magazines, they have pictures of John Malkovich, Glenn Close, and Michelle Pfeiffer next to me," Michael says of the publicity the film got early on. "They're not comparing it to the book."

There have been five film versions of the book by Choderlos de Laclos: *Les Liaisons Dangereuses*, by Roger Vadim in 1959; *Valmont*, with Annette Bening in 1989; a teenage version called *Cruel Intentions* in 1999; and another with the same title as the book featuring Rupert Everett and Catherine Deneuve in 2003, which is the most recent and, Michael feels, the most horrifying version. But everyone remembers the 1988 version with Glenn Close, "Because those performances were terrific. The cast was so terrific, and the production was so skilled. And basically we were going for the same kind of thing—great locations, great furniture, great surroundings, costumes, performances—because that's what they had, and so that's what we did. We wanted it to look beautiful, and chic, and glamorous."

Michael brought the story into the modern world and superimposed it onto New York's rabidly aggressive world of high fashion. "It's a very fashionable story with the theme of revenge, and I was thinking that this whole intrigue with *Dangerous Liaisons* in today's New York fashion world just fits perfectly. In fashion, people hate each other and want to destroy each other just as much as they want to destroy each other in Choderlos de Laclos's book."

Michael says he wanted a big movie that would give Lucas Entertainment the opportunity to dictate the market. A production as big as *Dangerous Liaisons* can push all of Michael's other productions with it, "and more power to the one who has the best product." Lucas Distribution is relatively new, but has already been incredibly successful. Although the number is small, there are some stores and distributors who are not buying from Lucas Entertainment, but such outlets will no longer be able to ignore Michael's company with respect to the handling of his product.

Although Michael's successful distribution company has had few challenges, the production of the current project developed its own set of roadblocks. "The biggest production challenge was drama with locations." In two cases, Michael's team had trouble the day before they were supposed to be shooting at particular locations. "There is a conductor named Jonathan Sheffer," says Michael. "He's a bad conductor, but is a millionaire. He has a lot of money. He and his boyfriend Christopher offered us the opportunity to shoot in their beautiful house."

The only condition was not the money, just that they

could watch it. Michael agreed. The next day, Sheffer asked for a $1,500 deposit, because it was the amount of the deductible for Michael's location insurance. Michael gave him a check. Then, two days before the production, Sheffer asked for a $10,000 security deposit, said Michael couldn't film the art on the walls, and that they wouldn't move it. The team would just have to work around it, which would have been impossible. Sheffer and his partner wouldn't talk about it with Michael and his team, saying they would have to discuss it all with Sheffer's manager in Los Angeles. "They didn't tell me any of this personally. They gave me all this information through their houseboy, who was incredibly arrogant and rude" (read more on the Web site blog for Sunday 02/06/05, www.DangerousLiaisonsXXX.com).

The second challenge was also with location. Michael had to switch locations to the house of one of his good friends. The friend's co-op gave the film team problems because they saw the camera, and someone told them Michael's team was filming. The rules of the co-op is that you have to ask permission first, but the co-op said it would be okay as long as the neighbor on the same floor would be fine with it. "The neighbor happened to be my dentist, who has done dental work for me and my whole family. He is gay, of course, and has two kids from surrogate mothers and a young boyfriend. I called him and said I would consider myself lucky because you are my dentist, and you know me, and that you'll call the co-op and tell them that it will be fine."

The dentist said it bothered him a little that they would be filming porn in the same building with his children. "I told him that my crew and my guys are much farther away from your children—all the way across a hall—than your bedroom where you and your boyfriend have sex, and your kids wouldn't even be there all afternoon." The dentist told Michael everything would be fine, but he called the co-op and lied to them that his boyfriend was coming out of the elevator and saw naked guys when the door opened. However, the team had only filmed dialogues on that day—no nude or sex scenes, and the elevator doors had never opened.

"We never had trouble from the straight crowd. But twice we had trouble from gay people who live and work in Chelsea and who watch porn. This is weird in a very gross way," Michael says. "I, of course, changed dentists after that. But the biggest challenges were from gay people who fucked us up, and we had nothing but support from straight people. That's very interesting."

Gay porn is forever changing. One of the keys to Michael's success is that he has been able to grow and change with the trends (along with setting a few of those trends himself). Audiences have recently become interested in hearing porn stars talking, having dialogue, and acting. Michael felt he had to accommodate that with a plot-driven film. "Also, people who work with me are very creative, very interesting people," says Michael. "And I decided I wanted to let these people express themselves." Michael says it was a joy to see them staying late, being enthusiastic, thinking about the project day and night, and coming up with great ideas. "It's incredible. It gave me the opportunity to appreciate the people I work with more, and to appreciate my own talent to get the most talented people together, and to hire the most talented people and make the right choices." In fact, Michael says that his best strength lies in this ability.

For Michael, it is not about the fact that he is a great director or that he is a great performer. "I don't direct sex so much. I think one of the talents I have is to put hot people together and make sure that I know first what they really like." This is why the scenes are so smooth, and it feels as if they're not directed, that they're natural. It is because they are. "After I talk to the guys, I know how to match them right. As an actor, I'm good, but I'm a good top actor. I prefer my actors to be versatile, so I treasure other actors more than I treasure myself as an actor."

Prior to *Dangerous Liaisons*, the largest budget for a gay porn film was $200,000. "This production may be a $250,000 project. I don't know; the numbers will come. But it's worth it to see what these people can do. And I'm proud that I got them together." Michael supports the creativity of his cast and crew because he feels it is important for them to feel good about their work. "Just to do porn, a stick-in-pull-out thing, is not something you can really be satisfied with, at least not my people. Sometimes it's not just about making a porn flick to make money. It's also about creating some form of art, and that's what they've brought to this project. I'm proud that I have people who are true artists."

Michael is proud of his team. His camera crew includes Tony DiMarco, who worked for Sony for thirteen years, and Raymond Dragon. "The team was huge," Michael says. It included two set stylists, three production assistants, a wardrobe stylist, and two photographers, just to name a few. "You know, when you look at all that work which was done, when you see the movie, when you see the photos, you can see what a great team I got for this production. It's the key to my success."

Michael also credits his cast as a key to his success. "I got Gus Mattox, who is a good performer and great actor, and has a Broadway background. He's done a lot of Broadway shows. We have Kent Larson, who is a great performer and a very good actor. I gave Wilfried Knight an English coach so he would lose his accent a bit. But everybody was just great in the production. Everybody acted very well, and it was a pleasure."

Michael is trying to find models whom he can sign on as

Lucas Entertainment exclusives. For the second time, he has signed a very exclusive agreement with a model. "My main model is Wilfried Knight, after myself. Now I've found another one, Bruce Beckham." Michael met Bruce working at the Food Bar, a popular restaurant in New York City. For three years, Michael asked Beckham to perform for him. He doesn't usually spend that much time wooing models, but with Beckham, was sure he would be a success story. "He has such an amazing body. He's absolutely stunning. His face is just unbelievable, absolutely gorgeous smile, big dick; everything is great."

Michael is very specific when it comes to what makes a porn star successful, and he has empirical evidence to back up his formula for success. On the other hand, he also is very specific about how a porn star can ruin his career. Rob Ramos and Wilson Vasquez have both modeled for Michael in films. "Wilson Vasquez was not interested in becoming a star. He is bisexual, and his girlfriend would forbid him to do movies. In the other case, Rob Ramos, he's a drug addict. So that was not possible."

Michael says that it is very difficult to find models like Wilfried Knight and Bruce Beckham, who are not only great physically, but who have great discipline. "They are in the gym every day, working hard, hard, hard. They are absolutely devoted to what they're doing. They're interested in making it work the best way." Michael says these two top guys know what they have to do for public appearances, to sign pictures and give interviews, and says they haven't needed any coaching from him on how to handle themselves in public or with the media. "I work with interesting guys. Wilfried Knight has a great life story. He has a law degree, just as I have. He had leukemia and beat it. He got in incredible shape after that, and five years later, he looks amazing."

Michael cannot stress enough how difficult it is to find a

model who has what it takes. "It is incredibly difficult to find someone who can have the whole look—beautiful body, big dick, great ass, killer face, great attitude, desire to become a huge star and be on top, and be patient, disciplined, drug-free, to have charisma, and to have brains." But, as he says himself, Michael's biggest talent is being able to find the very best and bring them together.

Michael has appeared on nearly 100 magazine covers over the years, but the bulk of his exposure has occurred over the past year and a half. Michael attributes this attention to the fact that he can "finally speak English." Also, people aren't interested in just a porn performer. Audiences are interested in a person they can talk to and identify with. Michael has a good relationship with all the publications, and is well liked among journalists and magazine feature writers.

In addition to his mutually respectful rapport with the media, Michael says that the photographers he works with produce such high-quality work that it is difficult for magazines to resist putting that quality on their covers. "I work only with fashion photographers—good name photographers. They do not necessarily want to be credited, but I work with them and pay them. They work with me, which is great, and it's a great quality cover."

Dangerous Liaisons is a big name—a recognizable name. "It's a big production with lots of comments from stars like RuPaul and a lot of different characters from downtown Manhattan." This kind of attention is giving Lucas Entertainment mainstream exposure. The press is gathering around Michael Lucas—journalists from *Genre*, *Instinct*, *Advocate*, *HX*, and television stations. "And that means mainstream opportunity." But with the highest budget in gay porn history, the culmination of artistic talent from all aspects of film production, attention from mainstream media, and classic source material, Michael knows that it still comes down to sex. The goal has been to raise industry standards. "The sex is five-star. I will never forget about what it's all for, but the connection between scenes is incredible. The energy, the story, everything just looks so great. The locations are gorgeous. Everyone is dressed in designers, put together by a very talented stylist. Altogether, it's a terrific result."

Another terrific result is the way the industry responded to the film. After years of Michael's award nominations and wins dwindling visibly—to Michael and to everyone else—*Dangerous Liaisons* finally gave him the recognition his body of work deserves. With thirteen GayVN award nominations, Michael took home the gold for *Dangerous Liaisons*. The film ended up winning four of its thirteen nods, including Best Picture, Best Supporting Actor for Kent Larson, Best Screenplay for Tony DiMarco, and Best DVD Extras/Special Edition.

41

Since the success of *Dangerous Liaisons*, much of what has kept Michael Lucas busy can be seen on his blog (www.LucasBlog.com). Keeping with the same formula for *Dangerous*, Michael sent out an open casting call on his blog for another big production, *La Dolce Vita*. On May 4, 2006, Michael blogged the tantalizing headline, "Take Part in Michael Lucas's *La Dolce Vita*!" The body of the entry then proceeded to ask for people with access to locations such as bars, apartments, lofts, and studios as well as extras to contact the company.

Also in keeping with the same formula as *Dangerous Liaisons*, Michael planned to set his new film around the New York fashion world, and scheduled shooting to start in September 2006 to coincide with fashion week. With such distinct parallels between the two films, lesser directors might fall into the trap of making the same film twice. However, if anyone can pull off two porn films in the same setting, that director is Michael Lucas. This is clearly evidenced by the success of the *Fire Island Cruising* series.

Because of this, Michael has years of experience at taking similar scenarios and not only keeping them fresh, but actually making them original and making them his own.

Fire Island was a hot spot for decades before Michael Lucas showed up, but has become branded in conjunction with the Lucas name. Clearly, Michael's next kingdom to conquer is fashion. His background in the fashion industry, from his experience in the fashion industry of Russia to being a slave to fashion, makes it a conquest worth the effort for Michael Lucas. But it is not just business that Michael discusses—rants about—in the daily dose of diva that his infamous blog has become.

Michael's blog is, on the surface, provocative and controversial. His opinions are often not popular, but are well educated, and they often come from a place of loyalty to the gay community. Is Michael always right? No. He is also not always nice, but he is never, ever apologetic. His blog bares his neck to the dogs the same way this very text does. It is his willingness to fight to the death that keeps him coming out on top. And thanks to the Internet, he does it daily.

42

Michael Lucas is very happy with his business because there are so few people who have what he has. He's not the type to get depressed because he's not Gwyneth Paltrow or Tom Cruise, because he realizes there are a handful of people out of millions who get to that level. "I have a great life," Michael says. "I have my niche. I have loads of people who admire me. I'm very successful on my level. I have money, I travel the world, I have thousands of fans—probably hundreds of thousands of fans. I'm on the cover of so many magazines; I'm being interviewed weekly. I'm respected, and they write about me all the time. So I'm very happy with my professional life, with the recognition I'm getting.

"Thank God, I don't work in a bar. Thank God, I had the balls to do what I'm doing. And that I'm so good at it that I actually could meet all these great people, and hang out with great, talented people—wise people, interesting people. Thank God, I made the right decision in my life.

"I'm very happy with my choice. I'm very happy that I came to this country, that I made it. I've had an interesting life, interesting experiences—coming from Moscow, then going through the whole immigrant experience, then being

illegal, to being popular, and now being the president of
my own company with fourteen American men working
for me on a daily basis. I hire hundreds of people every
year, freelancers from actors to models, to assistants and
cameramen and photographers. That makes me feel very
good. I pay the taxes and their salaries, and that makes me
feel great.

"I'm very happy with what I have, but I'll always look
for more. I'm always doing something different. I was a hustler; I became a company owner. I've got my production
company, my distribution company. I've started interviewing people, and that's become a production, interviewing
celebrities.

"I'm always into something new and interesting, and
I'm always growing. That's very good. Usually when someone is a hustler, he stays a hustler. But from that, I've found
ways of transforming myself and finding new abilities. I'm
very proud. I identify myself as a gay Jewish New Yorker, and
porn producer would be somewhere else. I guess I would
say gay, Jewish, upper-middle-class New Yorker. I'm not a
typical porn star. I'm very different by many means."

If Michael could sum up his life in one sentence, it
would be, "I always got what I wanted." His high school
friend, Anna, agrees that this represents Michael well. "He
could get everything he really wanted, but he didn't want
much. But things that interested him, he could always get.
It wasn't always easy, but he could. It wasn't about money
in Russia when we were young; it was about connections.
I don't even know what else."

"Of course, I have regrets," Michael says. "I regret that
I didn't come to America right away from Russia. I regret
that I didn't start making movies earlier. I regret that I didn't
bring my parents here, actually that I didn't convince them
to move out of Russia earlier, because my mother would be
in much better shape if I would have been able to get them

to come even a year earlier than they came. Things would be so much better with her health. So I have a lot of regrets. Everybody who is normal has regrets, and I do, too."

But the way he runs his business and his life are not part of those regrets. He will continue wielding his iron fist and razor-sharp tongue wherever necessary, demanding the best from those around him, and representing the GLBT community with pride and competence.

Michael recently donated money to the Gay and Lesbian Alliance Against Defamation (GLAAD) Media Awards, and was invited by his friend Will, an openly gay house-mate from the reality series *Big Brother,* to walk with him on the red carpet. Photographers went crazy upon sight of Will with gay porn star Michael Lucas! Later, about ten photographs from the red carpet appeared on GLAAD's Web site. However, the next day they were taken off the Web site, inexplicably—not only the pictures of Michael, and of Will and Michael together, but also those of just Will. The message this action sent was clear: Don't hang out with gay porn stars, or we will erase you.

Michael sent an e-mail to Joan Garry, who at the time was president of GLAAD. The e-mail began by explaining in a very pragmatic way that it was not GLAAD's position, as an organization dedicated to fair representation of gay people, to impose moral statements like the one made by the removal of Michael's pictures.

Michael went on to remind Garry that he has a history of being active in the gay community, and donating money and time to GLBT causes. He informed her that he campaigns heavily against drug abuse, particularly the abuse of crystal meth, and that he even goes so far as to drug test all of the performers who participate in his films. Porn actors who use drugs cannot work for Lucas Entertainment. He also told her of his advocacy for safe sex.

Then the trajectory of the e-mail changed. Michael told

Garry he was aware of GLAAD's decision to remove the photos of him at the award ceremony from GLAAD's Web site. He knew that GLAAD representatives had said they were embarrassed that he had come to the event.

Michael had donated $500 to the event, and felt it was hypocritical of GLAAD to accept the money, yet feel embarrassed by his presence on the red carpet.

"I want to say that I take great pride in my work," Michael said in the e-mail to Garry. "You may not agree with it; you may not like it (although I suspect many of you do). But it is an honest profession. I go to work every day and pay my taxes like everyone else."

Michael then suggested to Garry that GLAAD, an organization that is supposed to stop discrimination, should itself not discriminate against members of its own community. Michael assured Garry that he would continue to contribute money to the organization, but made it clear that their practice of internalized discrimination in this case was antithetical to their purpose.

After sending the e-mail, Michael called Garry and threatened to send the same e-mail to everyone—all the major publications, and to the 100,000 people on his e-mail list, and to all his fans. Its choice was to either put the photos back, and all its corporate sponsors would find out that it had a porn star on the red carpet, and they will pull their support—or perhaps the sponsors wouldn't mind at all—or face the consequences of Michael's letter.

The photos returned to GLAAD's Web site.

"Whoa," said Garry. "We didn't know that the pictures were off; that's not our policy. We're sorry about that. We don't know who did it. Can you give me the name of the person who told you that we said to take the pictures down?"

"No," Michael said. "You, as far as I can see, punish people for taking people with them on the red carpet. I will not give you my contacts. You'll fire the poor guy. Because a friend of mine told me that they said the pictures should be taken down because he's a porn star, and we're embarrassed."

Michael maintains the point that he made in his address to the students at Yale—gay people are different. "It's nice to be different," he says. "It's nice to be a little peculiar." The lesson that Michael taught GLAAD, and the lesson that many gay people could stand to learn, is that the richness of our diversity—even among our own community—is one of our greatest strengths.

Michael Lucas is, without hesitation, proud of his career and the success he has earned in it—and deservedly so. He lives his life and runs his business professionally, generously, compassionately, and honorably. He single-handedly validates the worth of the gay porn industry by doing it without shame or apology. This is how everyone can assign value to his life no matter what he is doing. The legacy of Michael Lucas is, be the best, and be proud of it.

That, ladies and gentlemen, is how dignity is done.

Michael Lucas
Filmography

Apartments
Auditions, Volume 1
Auditions, Volume 2
Auditions, Volume 3
Auditions, Volume 4
Auditions, Volume 5
Auditions, Volume 6
Auditions, Volume 7
Auditions, Volume 8
Auditions, Volume 9
Auditions, Volume 10
Back in the Saddle
Barcelona Nights
*Basic Plumbing 2 **
*The Chosen **
Director's Uncut
Encounters—At Your Service
Encounters—The Point of No Return
Fire Island Cruising
Fire Island Cruising 2
Fire Island Cruising 3
Fire Island Cruising 4

Fire Island Cruising 5
Fire Island Cruising 6
Fire Island Cruising 7
Fire Island Cruising 8
*High Tide**
Inside Paris
La Dolce Vita
Lifestyles
Lost
Lucas on Top
Manhattan Heat
*Maximum Cruise**
Michael Lucas' Dangerous Liaisons
Pick of the Pack
*Red Alert**
Straight to Prague
Stranger of the Night
To Moscow with Love
To Moscow with Love 2
Top to Bottom
Uncovered
Vengeance
Vengeance 2

* Indicates films credited as Michel Lucas for Falcon Studios.

Epilogue

At the onset of this project, Michael Lucas was completely involved with the book. He was very interested in telling his story because I had brought the idea to him and convinced him that it was a story worth telling.

For eight months, Michael worked tirelessly with me, participating in hour after hour of personal interviews which resulted in a very well-rounded account of his personal and professional life. Michael was interested in exposing his strengths as well as his flaws. He was able to reflect very clearly on his past in ways that were often very objective, almost to the point of dissociation. He gave me unfettered access to his friends, his family, his professional network of contacts, and even his enemies.

At a certain point, however, he began to distance himself from the project somewhat as if he was losing interest. After I had finished conducting the interviews about his life and his business and began working on the text itself, I seemed to lose contact with Michael. I tried very hard to keep him excited about it, but ultimately he made the decision to stop participating in the writing of the book. It is possible that he felt that his continued involvement with the book would appear self-serving, as if the point of the book was a publicity stunt (which was suggested by Chi Chi LaRue), but that is only conjecture. The point is that he withdrew his support of the biography.

The book does tend to portray him in a very flattering light. I have to confess, however, that his absence from the project had me tempted to slant the story in a different direction, but that would have been false. What I have reported about Michael and what he has stated in his own words on these pages portray him realistically. Professionally, he is truly the best in his business. That can't be changed. For the gay community, he is unfailingly supportive and he is avidly protective of all of us. Personally, he has strengths and flaws like the rest of us. The best and worst of those are captured here.

If this text flatters him, then I can only say it is an example of him. I am sorry that, for whatever reasons, Michael felt the need to depart from the project. But before he left, he held nothing back. That exposure is evidenced on every page, and for his honesty, if for nothing else, he is due my respect. He has it without reservation.

For every characteristic we may share with Michael, or are in opposition with him, he is in many ways a paragon of the gay community. Michael's views about politics are the same values by which he runs his business. He is well read and stays current on politics by reading *The New York Times* every day. "I'm very much interested in politics," Michael says. "They fascinate me, and they disgust me. I'm interested in what's going on in America, and the world. I have strong opinions, and some of my opinions are not very popular. I always support the Democratic party because it's the best we have of the two. I don't agree with everything they do, because I'm not for the larger government.

"I'm for smaller government, and I'm more capitalist than socialist. I think America is great because it is such a capitalist country. And I think that capitalism is the only way to go; there's nothing better. But Republicans are much more religious than Democrats, and I cannot stand anything about religion."

When Michael was growing up in Russia, he seemed to be rebelling against the country's atheism by attending synagogue with Ivanna and Anna. Here, he rebels against right-wing conservative religion in politics. While this may seem contradictory, it is not for two reasons. First, going to synagogue for him, as he explained clearly, was not about religion. It was all about Jewish culture. Second, it is just as wrong to force religion as it is to forbid it. "Religion and state should be kept separate," Michael says.

"As a gay man, I support Democrats much more than Republicans because they are more pro-gay than Republicans," Michael says. "I don't have a favorite politician. I will vote for Hillary Clinton if she runs for President in 2008. I saw a lot of her speeches. I was at a lot of her dinners. Whenever there was money involved, she would attend dinners for gay people. At the same time, she never did anything really for gay people, in my opinion. It's very difficult for gay people to reach her and get her involvement unless it's some kind of fund-raiser; then she'll be right there.

"But she is a great speaker. She impressed me very much. She's idolized by gay people—not only by gay people, but by many people. She's a very smart woman. Will she betray gay people when she's in office? I'm sure, just like her husband. Will she be a little better than her husband? Maybe she will be, because time changes. At least she wouldn't be so outrageous like Bush. She wouldn't go on television and say that we have to save the sanctity of marriage. It would be great just not to hear something like that.

"I think it would be very banal for me to talk about

George W. Bush, because we all hate him. He's a marionette in the hands of horrible people—homophobes." Even though Michael said in his address to the students at Yale that he doesn't think this administration will go after pornographers, he realizes that it is a very real threat and hopes that it does not happen.

One of the leading people in the fight to ban pornography is Andrea Dworkin. However, her own words betray her attempt to make a sound, intelligent argument. In her book *Pornography: Men Possessing Women*, she tries to define the word "pornography" using etymology, and states that "It means the graphic depiction of women as vile whores."

This simply is not true. The etymology of the word "pornography" means, "the writing of prostitutes." Historically, prostitutes who worked in brothels made money on volume. The more clients they were able to see, the more money they could make. So they took to writing sexual things and posting sexual photographs on the walls of their rooms in order to speed up the process for each of their clients. They would be more turned on seeing the sexually explicit words and pictures, and they got off faster. So the prostitute was able to serve more clients and make more money. It's that simple.

So, Dworkin's "definition" is either an error of fact, or simply a lie perpetuated in the interest of propaganda against porn. I have developed a more accurate definition of pornography that takes into account its etymology, its original uses and intents, and its more contemporary uses and intents. Pornography is the documentation of sexuality in images, text, film, music, or other media, produced with the intention of human sexual arousal.

While there are examples of harm that can result from exposure to pornography, it is irrational to advocate the elimination of its production because there are also many benefits that result from pornography as well as an undeniable social value that is gained from its continued existence. The threshold of what is deemed acceptable by society changes with time, and by subjection to different and repeated stimuli, such as those found in pornography. Although this position has been used by those who take a stand against pornography as an argument that pornography is destructive, it is this very statement that indicates the social value of pornography. To illustrate this point, it is first necessary to challenge the argument that pornography is destructive, and apply examples to the definition of pornography.

Along with Dworkin, Catharine MacKinnon has been on the forefront of the position to ban pornography of any kind. In her book *Only Words*, she suggests that pornography objectifies and dehumanizes women by saying, "With pornography, by contrast, consumers see women as less than human." However, Hegel's description of humanity negates MacKinnon's assumption. In *Phenomenology of Spirit*, Hegel states, "This other is *for itself* only when it supersedes itself as being for itself, and is for itself only in the being-for-self of the other." In simpler terms, Hegel is saying that we can only recognize ourselves by how we appear in the eyes of others. It is only by how we view others that we are able to define ourselves. This is objectification and, as Hegel states, is necessary for the recognition of our own humanity. It is impossible for objectification to be "dehumanizing" when it is an essential part of the human condition.

The person being objectified, or slave as described by Hegel, is in a way the master in that he or she is essential to the master. This dynamic of Hegel's master-slave dialectic is portrayed flawlessly in the film *The Secretary*. The character of the secretary is certainly having needs met by getting spanked, and is somewhat in control of the situation by knowing she can get what she needs from the at-torney character by making typing errors, and by present-ing him with worms and bugs. MacKinnon fails to see the possibility of a person being able to value such a dual po-sition of submission and power. However, MacKinnon's use of the word "consumers" is interesting.

It signifies that pornography benefits society because it is good for economics. In *The Pornography Controversy*, Peter Michelson states, "The way, therefore, to make the world safe for pornography is to show it that sex is good for business." This single statement is true on a number of levels. First of all, the sex industry generates billions of dollars of revenue every year in the United States alone. This kind of consumer activity not only shows the demand for pornography but also shows that many more people use pornography than are willing to admit it.

Second, this statement speaks of current advertising trends. The idea that "sex sells" is not a new idea. It is wide-ly used in every consumer culture on the planet. It is so widely used because it works. Clothiers Abercrombie & Fitch have had to deal with controversy surrounding their catalogs that feature nudity. Sam Shahid, who has been in charge of Abercrombie & Fitch's advertising campaigns for a decade, insists that they are not selling clothes, they are selling an attitude. It is fun to be sexy, and sexual.

If being sexy and sexual is seen as problematic, that is just an example of the American culture of hypocrisy, which tells children that it is all right to rent movies with vio-lence, but not movies with nudity or sexual situations. Michelson also compares *Playboy* magazine to *Cosmopoli-tan* magazine. The comparison could be made to any other magazine. Advertising is produced with the intention of human sexual arousal, in an effort to bring recognition to a product being sold. According to my definition of porno-graphy, this type of advertising is pornographic, even if sex is not the commodity being sold. However, this is not a bad thing.

In *Civilization and Its Discontents*, Freud says, "Non-satisfaction is not so painfully felt in the case of instincts kept in dependence as in the case of uninhibited ones." This means that humans must have an outlet for aggression, including sexual aggression. These outlets are called *sublimation*, as Freud puts it, "shifting the instinctual aims in such a way that they cannot come up against frustration from the external world." In the same way that sublimation is a product of human nature, in an effort to sustain well-being, pornography is the man-made product of culture that enables humans to effectively ensure that well-being. The alternative to the pleasant and conscious choice of sublimation is repression. Repression is not a conscious choice, is unpleasant, and is indicative of what Freud calls a "neurotic," or a person who has not successfully sublimated unconscious desires.

Nadine Strossen, author of *Defending Pornography*, reinforces the idea of healthy sublimation by stating, "Sexually explicit materials may well be the only source of sexual information or pleasure for many people who, for a host of reasons, do not have sexual contact with others." There could be so many instances where a person might not have sexual contact with other people. Strossen indicates examples, such as people who are shy, people with disabilities, people isolated from others, and those who are gay but afraid to express their sexuality.

Just as these types of people were Michael Lucas's clients when he was escorting, the same kinds of people—as well as others with no such disabilities—are the ones who are now the customers of his pornography. Strossen quotes law professor Kathleen Sullivan, who wrote, "In a world where sodomy may still be made a crime, gay pornography is the samizdat of the oppressed." In Soviet Russia, samizdats were writings that had been officially banned, but that were circulated secretly.

Pornography as a form of sublimation brings forth a clear distinction between fantasy and reality. Sometimes those who view pornography want to participate in the types of activities that are being shown or described. However, this is often not the case, as Lucas stated in his address at Yale. Strossen says, "The distinction between the imagined and the actual, between fantasy and reality, should be crystal clear." This is one of many key elements in her work.

Another key element to Strossen's argument is that "women who voluntarily perform for pornography resent the procensorship feminists' attempts to outlaw their chosen occupation." It is impossible to say that every woman who participates in a porn film is coerced into it. No person is qualified to speak for every individual, as MacKinnon tries to do, just as it is impossible to say that every person who views pornography wants to participate in the types of activities he or she is seeing. It is this bravado, indicating some sort of false omniscience, that weakens the argument against pornography.

Another weakness in the argument against pornography is the reasoning fallacy behind the statement that pornography causes violent behavior. This is called the *post hoc ergo propter hoc* (after this therefore because of this) fallacy. Strossen states that this type of reasoning, "underscores the illogicality of presuming that just because two phenomena happen to coexist, they therefore are causally linked." Just because some violent people may view pornography does not indicate that pornography causes violence. If it was discovered that many serial killers used a certain brand of shampoo, it would be illogical in the same way to determine that this specific brand of shampoo caused people to commit serial homicide.

MacKinnon does not take gay porn into consideration when she makes the sweeping generalization that all porn objectifies women. It is impossible for a pornographic medium to objectify women when there are no women involved. However, the antipornography advocates attempt to do so. Strossen quotes John Preston's criticism of Andrea Dworkin. Dworkin wrote "THIS OPPRESSES WOMEN" on any medium that promoted male homosexuality. Preston's reaction to this is to say, "I've come to understand that it's the expression of *any* male sexuality that she feels fuels the oppression of women in our society." Preston's observation of Dworkin's behavior indicates that the pro-censorship feminist's intent is not to fight misogyny, but to promote misandry.

Strossen further states that "no censorship regime could completely suppress pornography. It would continue to exist underground." Making pornography illegal would not eliminate it. In the same way that the law would not stop abortions, it would simply make them dangerous; the law would not stop pornography. The only thing it would succeed in doing would be to remove the legal protections that are currently in place for those who work in the sex trade. And as Tim Campbell indicated in his testimony at the Minneapolis hearings, it would diminish the quality of the product being produced in a way that would encourage unsafe practices. This also applies to prostitution. Prostitution already exists. It always has and will. If prostitution were made legal, it could be made safer, and those who pursued it as a way to make a living could do so with less danger and stigma.

In 1992, the Canadian Supreme Court agreed with the feminist position against pornography, resulting in the *Butler* decision, which states, "[I]t is sufficient . . . for Parliament to have a reasonable basis for concluding that harm will result and this requirement does not demand actual proof of harm." This decision essentially has allowed the Canadian government to assign victimization to a victimless situation, and to criminalize pornography using the same post hoc reasoning that Strossen proves to be illogical. The same could happen if conservatives were able to get their hands on the regulation of pornography in the United States.

People like MacKinnon and Dworkin who want to ban pornography completely are clearly not making a strong enough case. Their flawed reasoning, combined with the relevant benefits of pornography, are the reasons that pornography will never be banned completely. The cause for concern lies instead in selective censorship, with certain people trying to decide which is acceptable and which is not. This puts gay porn at risk, a notion that is infuriating.

This concern has precedence under Canada's *Butler* decision. Strossen states that "any censorship measure would be enforced by government officials and legal systems that reflect society's pervasive homophobia and heterosexism." In Canada, it has been lesbian and gay pornography that has come under the most censorship fire. Strossen later states, "The more unconventional the sexual expression is, the more revolutionary its social and political implications become." However, Canada has proven a better commitment to the inclusion of its GLBT citizens by being one of five countries to allow gay marriage.

In this respect, the United States should have been the first to make this possible, or the Constitution is a lie. GLBT citizens of the United States are not equal. That piece of paper does not protect us, or include us. And it won't, until it also reads, "Equality of rights, under the law, shall not be denied or abridged by the United States, or by any state, on account of sexual orientation or gender identity."

Does this mean that all pornography should be allowed— that all pornography has the same social value? "Snuff" films are pornographic films produced where a subject is murdered for the sexual gratification of the other participant(s) of the film, and of the viewer. Some people worry that the films are not only too realistic, but that they are real, and that a person is actually getting murdered in order for these films to be produced.

Pornography itself does not objectify people; other people do. As Hegel states, it is the human condition. It is how we know we are alive, by objectifying, and by ourselves being objectified by others. Pornography is an expression of humanity and is the documentation of human sexuality. Human sexuality is many things. It can be fun, powerful, a way to procreate, a way to express love, a way to release tension or stress, a way to relax, to show dominance or submission, and much more.

And as the documentation of human sexuality, pornography is many things. It describes sexuality, informs, educates, provides an outlet for sublimation and fantasy, and much more. By my own definition, romance novels meet the criteria of pornography. Advertising definitely meets the criteria of pornography. Sex films and magazines featuring nude models and sexual situations are the most obvious forms of pornography. Certain music, with lyrics and tones designed for sexual arousal, also can fit the criteria for pornography.

But it is impossible to develop a set of criteria that would distinguish between "socially valuable" porn and "socially destructive" porn. Our responsibility is not to censor what is potentially valuable. Our responsibility is to minimize the effects of any harm caused by misuse, in a rational way, but not at the cost of what results from censorship and prohibition.

Strossen says that "the fact that pornography always has rebelled against conventional constraints is precisely the reason it has always provoked such anxiety." Human sexuality and the documentation of it have a certain power that clearly threatens patriarchal society, but they are essential and necessary. Sexuality is a part of who we are. Strossen goes on to say that "just as sex itself has enormous power to break down individual and social boundaries, so speech about sex threatens all manner of accepted bounds." Pornography moves boundaries, and therein lies its social value. We must push the threshold if individuals are to have an educated, valuable grasp of how to actually decide what is and is not acceptable for themselves. There is a word for moving the threshold of acceptance in order to embrace new things and ideas. It is growth.

Acknowledgments

First of all, I must thank Michael Lucas for giving me the opportunity to tell his story. Thank you for being so available to me and to the project.

Thanks to Emalei Koester for transcription assistance, and to Fallon Koester for transcription and research assistance. Thanks to everyone in Michael's office at Lucas Entertainment for providing me with every scrap and image I bugged you for, sometimes daily; I appreciate your patience with me. Thanks to Len Evans (sweetie, darling!) for putting me in touch with Michael in the first place. Thank you, David Ciminelli, for giving me a shot.

Thank you to Dr. Lissa Skitol for guiding me toward the perspective I have regarding pornography. Thanks to Dr. John Ronan for leading me to Butler, and to Dr. Leigh Anne Duck for—my God—everything. Tons of thanks to my agent, Jim Cypher, for working with me tirelessly, and for believing in me and in the project. To my editor, John Scognamiglio, your guidance and patience have brought me into this world so comfortably and professionally.

And thanks to all the people—friends and family of Michael—who so generously gave their time to being interviewed on behalf of this project. Those people are Lena

Treyvas (you are such a lady), Richard Winger, Jason Bellini, Rod Novoa, Gerald McCullouch (www.TheMomentAfter. net), Wilfried Knight, Kent Larson, Mickey Skee, Doug Oliver, Alan Cumming, Tim Valenti, Specialty Publications, T. Hitman, Mario Ortiz, Mark Adams, Anna Pobedinski, and Marina Giliver.
Thanks to . . .
John Rutherford
President, Creative Director
COLT Studio Group
P.O. Box 883694
San Francisco, CA 94188-3694
phone: 415-437-9800
fax: 415-437-9803
e-mail: john@COLTstudiogroup.com
www.COLTstudiogroup.com

Michael Lucas
President
Lucas Entertainment
101 West Twenty-Third Street
#2149
New York, NY 10011
phone: 212-924-5892
michael@LucasEntertainment.com

Bibliography

Boswell, James. *Boswell's Life of Johnson*. 1904. Oxford Standard Author's Edition. London: Oxford University Press, 1961.

Butler, Judith. *Antigone's Claim: Kinship Between Life and Death*. New York: Columbia University Press, 2000.

Butler, Judith. *Gender Trouble: Feminism and the Subversion of Identity*. New York: Routledge, 1990.

Dworkin, Andrea. *Pornography: Men Possessing Women*. New York: G.P. Putnam's Sons, 1979.

Freud, Sigmund. *Civilization and Its Discontents*. New York: W.W. Norton & Company, 1961.

Greenfield-Sanders, Timothy. *XXX: 30 Porn Star Portraits*. Boston: Bulfinch Press, 2004.

Hegel, G.W.F. *Phenomenology of Spirit*. New York: Oxford University Press, 1977.

MacKinnon, Catharine. *Only Words*. Cambridge: Harvard University Press, 1993.

MacKinnon, Catharine, and Andrea Dworkin, eds. *In Harm's Way: The Pornography Civil Rights Hearings*. Cambridge, MA: Harvard University Press, 1997.

Michelson, Peter. "The Pleasures of Commodity, or How to Make the World Safe for Pornography." *The Porno-*

graphy Controversy: Changing Moral Standards in American Life. New Brunswick, NJ: Transaction Books, 1975.

Orleck, Annelise. *The Soviet Jewish Americans.* Photographs by Elizabeth Cooke. Westport, CT: Greenwood Press, 1999.

Shasha, Dennis, and Marina Shron. *Red Blues: Voices from the Last Wave of Russian Immigrants.* New York: Holmes & Meier, 2002.

Strossen, Nadine. *Defending Pornography: Free Speech, Sex, and the Fight for Women's Rights.* New York: New York University Press, 1995.

Theophano, Teresa, ed. *Queer Quotes.* Boston: Beacon Press, 2004.